The 21ˢᵗ Century
Retirement Security Plan

The 21st Century Retirement Security Plan

Final Report of the
National Commission on Retirement Policy

CHAIRMEN
Senator Judd Gregg
Senator John Breaux
Representative Jim Kolbe
Representative Charles W. Stenholm
Donald B. Marron
Dr. Charles A. Sanders

EXECUTIVE DIRECTOR
Bradley D. Belt

ASSISTANT DIRECTOR
Greg D. Kubiak

MARCH 1999

About CSIS

The Center for Strategic and International Studies (CSIS), established in 1962, is a private, tax-exempt institution focusing on international public policy issues. Its research is nonpartisan and nonproprietary.

CSIS is dedicated to policy impact. It seeks to inform and shape selected policy decisions in government and the private sector to meet the increasingly complex and difficult global challenges that leaders will confront in the next century. It achieves this mission in three ways: by generating strategic analysis that is anticipatory and interdisciplinary; by convening policymakers and other influential parties to assess key issues; and by building structures for policy action.

CSIS does not take specific public policy positions. Accordingly, all views, positions, and conclusions expressed in this publication should be understood to be solely those of the authors.

Library of Congress Cataloging-in-Publication Data

The 21st century retirement security plan : the National Commission on Retirement Policy final report / Bradley D. Belt, editor.
      p. cm. — (CSIS panel reports, ISSN 0899–0352)
    Includes bibliographical references.
    ISBN 0–89206–353–X
    1. Retirement income—Government policy—United States. 2. Old age pensions—Government policy—United States. 3. Pension trusts—Government policy—United States. 4. Social security—United States. 5. Twenty-first century—Forecasts. I. Belt, Bradley D. II. National Commission on Retirement Policy. III. Center for Strategic and International Studies (Washington, D.C.). IV. Title: National Commission on Retirement Policy final report. V. Title: Twenty-first century retirement security plan. VI. Series.
HD7125.A123   1999   99–24204
331.25'2'0973—dc21   CIP

Comments are welcome and should be directed to:

Bradley D. Belt
National Commission on Retirement Policy
Center for Strategic and International Studies
1800 K Street, N.W.
Washington, D.C. 20006
Telephone: (202) 887-0200
E-mail: bbelt@csis.org
Web: http://www.csis.org

Contents

Dear Fellow Americans:

The National Commission on Retirement Policy (NCRP) is issuing the final report of its recommendations at a particularly critical time. The President and Congress have each publicly committed themselves not only to strengthening the Social Security program, but also to increasing retirement income for all Americans in the twenty-first century. Improved revenue projections for the federal budget provide a unique opportunity to set aside the necessary funds to ensure that future benefit promises are met. The question before us is whether there exists a true spirit of bipartisan cooperation and compromise needed to complete the job.

The attached report can serve as a road map for such reform. We commend this proposal to you not only for the policy goals it achieves, but also for the spirit of compromise it embodies. Our Commission included 24 experts on retirement policy from both the public and private sectors. These experts brought with them very diverse approaches to addressing the issue of retirement income security. After 15 months of work, last May the Commission voted unanimously to report the enclosed recommendations. Our success came about not because 24 members, or even one member, felt persuaded that every element of our proposal was the best one. It was, rather, that each of the 24 members of the Commission worked together in the spirit of cooperation and compromise to develop this plan.

Similar cooperation will be necessary if Congress and the president are to make the necessary choices to expand and solidify all sources of retirement income in the twenty-first century. We hope that, like the members of our Commission, members of Congress, and the administration will follow the model of compromise established by the NCRP and eschew rigid perspectives toward policy in the interest of completing this most important task—enhancing the retirement security for all Americans.

Naturally, any cooperative agreement on a comprehensive proposal to strengthen retirement security will require trade-offs and tough choices. Our proposal is no different. Although you may not agree with every part of this plan, we ask that you consider it in its entirety, including all it achieves, before making a judgment. Moreover, we encourage you to ask, "What other plan achieves as much?"

As the cochairs of the NCRP, we remain committed to advancing the ideas put forward in this proposal, and to continuing the effort to implement policies that will increase the retirement income available to Americans in the twenty-first century and beyond.

Sincerely,

Judd Gregg
United States Senate

John Breaux
United States Senate

Jim Kolbe
U.S. House of Representatives

Charles W. Stenholm
U.S. House of Representatives

Donald B. Marron
Chairman and CEO, Paine Webber Group, Inc.

Dr. Charles A. Sanders
Retired Chairman and CEO, Glaxo, Inc.

Preface and Acknowledgments

Tackling public policy challenges of the magnitude of restructuring the U.S. Social Security system requires vision, commitment, and, most of all, extraordinary leadership. These certainly were the qualities exhibited by the members of the National Commission on Retirement Policy (NCRP), especially its six cochairmen. They labored over a period of nearly a year and a half, reviewing an extensive record of information about Social Security, private pensions, and personal savings behavior; meeting with policy experts and interested constituencies; and engaging in hours of vigorous debate about the issues and appropriate policy responses.

The resulting product, the 21st Century Retirement Security Plan (the "Plan"), is a reflection of the tremendous amount of hard work put in by the members of the NCRP. It is a comprehensive, bipartisan, and intellectually rigorous proposal for addressing one of the most pressing public policy challenges facing the United States. It is a fiscally responsible, politically viable, and practically achievable approach to ensuring the long-term financial solvency of the Social Security system and enhancing retirement security for future generations of Americans.

The NCRP's Plan is a reflection as well of the spirit of cooperation and compromise that prevailed throughout its deliberations. Although the Plan was *unanimously* endorsed by the NCRP's membership—an extraordinary accomplishment itself—it is fair to say that not a single member would necessarily endorse each and every element of the Plan if considered separately. Ultimately, however, everyone agreed that the Plan—in its totality—meets all the objectives and principles established by the NCRP.

As is always the case in such undertakings, the successful outcome is due to the contributions of many people who labored tirelessly behind the scenes and without the public recognition they so richly deserve. Without their dedication, commitment, and extraordinary talents, none of this would have been possible. I especially want to acknowledge Greg Kubiak—the glue that held the NCRP together—Kim Klein, Mark Schoeff, and Paul Hewitt of the Center for Strategic and International Studies (CSIS); Chuck Blahous with the office of Senator Judd Gregg (R–N.H.); Michelle Prejean and Darla Romfo with the office of Senator John Breaux (D–La.); Brigitte Schmidt and Tori Gorman with the office of Representative Jim Kolbe (R–Ariz.); James Hamilton and Ed Lorenzen with the office of Representative Charlie Stenholm (D–Tex.); and Kathleen Shanahan and Jennifer Maldanado of Paine Webber. We owe them our deepest gratitude and appreciation.

The work of the NCRP would not have been possible without the generous support of, among others, the Scholl Foundation, the Pritzker Foundation, the J. M. Kaplan Fund, Paine Webber, Exxon, IBM, FMR Corp., American Express, Aetna, the American Council of Life Insurance, Citibank, and Dart Industries.

How the Social Security reform debate will unfold remains to be seen. Without question, however, CSIS's National Commission on Retirement Policy has performed a great public service by demonstrating there is a bipartisan solution that strengthens the Social Security system and enhances retirement security for all Americans.

Bradley D. Belt
Executive Director

Executive Summary

Introduction

Laying the foundation for economic growth and prosperity in the face of the profound demographic changes that will occur early in the next century is perhaps the most difficult challenge facing the United States. The imminent retirement of the "baby boom" generation, combined with longer life expectancies, will place extraordinary pressures on the economic resources necessary to sustain the rising standard of living that Americans have come to expect—and potentially fray the vital threads of the safety net programs the government provides for senior citizens.

Quite simply, we—as a country and as individuals—are ill-prepared to meet the financial challenges of the twenty-first century. We are confronted with a rapidly aging population, actuarially unsound federal health and retirement programs, unsustainable trends of spending for government programs for senior citizens, and inadequate levels of private savings. We have promised too much collectively and set aside too little individually. As a result, the proverbial "three-legged stool" of resources for retirement security—Social Security, private pension plans, and personal savings—that traditionally has financed Americans' retirement is increasingly unstable and in need of repair.

Last year, the National Commission on Retirement Policy (NCRP) published *Can America Afford to Retire?* a document that illustrates the inexorable demographic trends, enormous fiscal pressures, and insufficient personal savings that threaten future standards of living of aging Americans. The following findings warrant the attention and action of policymakers.

America Is Growing Older

Today, one in eight Americans is aged 65 or older. As the first wave of the baby boom generation will begin to retire after 2010 (early retirement for Social Security benefits would be 2008), however, the share of older Americans will increase significantly. By 2040, nearly one in four will be 65 or older. At the same time, life expectancy will continue to rise. On average, Americans are living 14 years longer than when Social Security was created, and the trend toward longer lifespans will continue. These demographic changes will place tremendous fiscal pressure on federal retirement and health programs for the elderly. Furthermore, a "baby bust" succeeded the baby boom—meaning that there will be fewer workers to help finance each retiree's benefits in the future.

We Have Promised Too Much

Federal entitlement programs—under which money is spent automatically on a category of recipients who meet government-specified qualifications—consume an ever-increasing share of our country's financial resources. Spending on entitlements (principally federal health and retirement programs) has more than doubled since 1963 and now accounts for almost half of federal outlays. By the government's own estimates, at the current rate of federal spending entitlements could absorb all government revenues by 2030.

We Are Saving Too Little

As a country and as individuals, we are not saving enough to meet future consumption needs. The rate of personal savings has declined steadily over the past few decades and now is approaching historic lows—insufficient to meet the future retirement needs of most Americans. Although recent gains in financial markets have buoyed a sense of wealth in many Americans, current annual individual savings rates are near zero. In fact, Americans, as a whole, actually had negative savings rates (as a percentage of disposable income) for the months September and October 1998, according to the U.S. Department of Commerce, the first negative monthly national savings rates since the agency began keeping such statistics more than 40 years ago.[1] Low savings not only threatens the ability of individuals to retire with financial security, it also reduces the pool of capital available for investment, the pool that creates jobs and economic growth—all essential elements of higher standards of living for all Americans.

These Trends Are Unsustainable

Without significant public policy and social responses to the impending challenges, the standard of living for retirees after the first quarter of the twenty-first century could decline. Society simply will be unable to afford all the promises we have made absent change. A failure to act boldly with structural reforms now will raise future costs dramatically and require added sacrifices 10 to 20 years down the road. All policymakers who have examined the issue recognize both the need for action and the benefits of acting sooner rather than later.

The Social Safety Net

Presently, inflows to the Social Security system exceed benefits paid out. The program's Trust Fund will begin to pay out more in benefits than it collects in payroll taxes soon after the baby boomers begin retiring, however, and will run even larger annual operating deficits thereafter. According to the Social Security trustees, if no action is taken in the interim, the Trust Fund will be entirely depleted

---

1. U.S. Department of Commerce, Bureau of Economic Analysis, "Personal Income and Outlays," BEA *News Release,* October 1998.

by 2032. Because of these trends, polls show young people are losing faith in the system.

Private Retirement Plans

Currently, fewer than half of all workers are enrolled in an employer-sponsored pension plan. The problem is even more acute for those working in small businesses. As of 1993, 84 percent of workers in companies employing more than 1,000 people had access to a retirement plan, but only 17 percent of workers in companies with 25 or fewer employees had a retirement plan available to them at work. As a result, only about 20 percent of Americans in businesses with 100 or fewer employees participate in a retirement plan. The problem is worse for women and minorities who tend to have shorter job tenures and who are more likely to be part-time employees without coverage by an employer-sponsored plan. Moreover, current pension rules allow for excessive leakage and can be overly complex and burdensome.

Personal Savings

As they do now, retirees will have to supplement Social Security payments with personal savings. Financial experts tell us, however, that current levels of personal retirement savings are not nearly adequate to ensure financial independence for most Americans when they retire—even *with* pension and Social Security payments. The rate of personal savings fell from almost 12 percent of gross domestic product (GDP) in 1965 to about 5 percent of GDP in 1995 and has continued to decline. According to one study by Merrill Lynch, the oldest baby boomers are saving just one-third of what they will need to maintain their current standard of living during retirement. The fact is that most American families have very little set aside to meet future retirement expenses.

Addressing the Challenge

Because we have over-promised when it comes to the future benefits of the Social Security system, the level of Social Security benefits for future retirees will come under increased scrutiny. This is evidenced by the attention Social Security has received from President Bill Clinton, leaders in Congress, think tanks, academics, and the media.

Increasingly, Americans are arriving at the realization that Social Security alone will not assure a secure retirement, and that reliance on the limited resources of the federal government brings with it an increasing degree of risk. Individuals will have to assume greater personal responsibility for their own retirement security. The responsibility of Congress and the administration, therefore, not only is to restore Social Security's actuarial solvency, but also to develop a comprehensive and integrated approach to retirement security by strengthening all areas of retirement savings. This not only will help to ensure an adequate standard of living for future generations of retirees, but will also foster continued economic growth and prosperity for the country.

The National Commission on Retirement Policy

The Center for Strategic and International Studies (CSIS) established the bipartisan National Commission on Retirement Policy (the "Commission") at the beginning of 1997 to highlight the looming retirement security challenge and recommend comprehensive and politically viable solutions to meet it. The 24-member Commission is composed of respected and knowledgeable leaders from both the public and private sectors.

In its mission statement, the Commission outlined three primary objectives:

❏ to educate the American public about the scope and magnitude of the retirement financing challenge;

❏ to provide the foundation for nonpartisan and informed policy debate; and

❏ to build a national consensus for the changes necessary to place the country on a sound, long-term fiscal footing and ensure a secure retirement for all Americans.

The Commission also established three guiding principles in the beginning of its deliberative process:

❏ National retirement policy should be designed to enable Americans to enjoy a reasonable standard of living in their retirement years. National retirement policy should encompass government programs that require a floor of financial support for elderly retirees and initiatives that encourage and facilitate group (that is, employer) and individual savings to provide additional retirement income above the floor of support;

❏ National retirement policy should contribute to long-term growth and economic prosperity; and

❏ Government programs for elderly retirees should be financially sound and economically sustainable. The costs of financing these programs and other initiatives that encourage and facilitate national saving should be borne equitably between and among generations.

During the course of the subsequent 15 months, the Commission held several public meetings and fact-finding hearings and met with a wide range of interested constituencies, including business, labor, and seniors groups as part of an aggressive information gathering and outreach effort.

The 21st Century Retirement Security Plan

The result of the Commission's 18-month deliberative effort is the 21st Century Retirement Security Plan. The Plan is unique in its bipartisan, comprehensive approach to retirement security, which encompasses improvements and reforms to all three principal sources of retirement savings: Social Security, private pensions, and personal savings. The interdependence of these areas cannot be ignored. The

Key Elements of the 21st Century Retirement Plan

- Directs 2 percent of the current payroll tax into individual security accounts (ISAs) modeled on the Thrift Savings Plan;
- Allows for additional voluntary contributions to the ISA up to $2,000;
- Provides different investment alternatives;
- Strengthens the safety net by creating additional antipoverty protections within the traditional Social Security system;
- Gradually raises the eligibility age for full retirement benefits;
- Establishes a universal salary reduction–qualified retirement plan available to all employers;
- Moves to a universal income limit for IRAs;
- Makes it possible for workers to move retirement benefits among employer-sponsored plans;
- Creates catch-up provisions for individuals who have been without a pension plan for five years or longer;
- Provides cost-effective defined-benefit alternatives for small employers; and
- Reduces the time it takes for employers' matching contributions to vest.

more Americans save and invest through private pensions and personal savings, the more capital will be available to fuel growth and to provide the government with more options to ensure the stability of the Social Security system.

The 21st Century Retirement Security Plan meets the goals established by the NCRP for Social Security. The Plan would:

❏ restore the long-term solvency of Social Security (OASDI);

❏ provide the traditional OASDI program with a stable Trust Fund at the end of the actuarial valuation period, so that the passage of time will not affect adversely measures of solvency;

❏ increase the retirement income provided through Social Security relative to traditional means of restoring the program to solvency;

❏ reduce significantly long-term debt and liabilities of the federal government to Social Security;

❏ enable Social Security to lift more of the elderly out of poverty than current law does;

❏ add incentives for individuals to remain in the workforce longer, thereby improving worker-to-beneficiary ratios;

❏ create individual savings accounts within Social Security that provide individuals with ownership and control over the investment of a portion of their Federal Insurance Contributions Act (FICA) taxes;

❑ enhance opportunities for providing retirement security through private
pension plans and personal savings, and

❑ accomplish all the above objectives without a tax increase and without
placing an additional mandatory savings requirement on employers or
employees.

Social Security Reforms

The NCRP Plan would modernize the Social Security system to allow individuals
more personal choice and greater growth potential for their funds through the
creation of individual security accounts (ISAs), funded by payroll tax
contributions. The Plan also would keep Social Security solvent for the next 70
years without tax increases; improve benefits for lower-income workers and
establish higher minimum benefit levels to help the most vulnerable in our society;
and encourage seniors to continue working by allowing them to keep their earnings
without offsetting their Social Security benefits. Under the NCRP's Plan, a single
person retiring at age 65 could reasonably expect to receive in the year 2030 an
increase of nearly 10 percent in his or her retirement income as compared with
traditional approaches to achieving solvency (such as raising payroll taxes or
cutting benefits). An individual retiring at age 67 in 2060, in fact, could expect a
38.4 percent increase.

Private Pension Plans and Personal Retirement Savings Reforms

The private pension and personal retirement savings legs of the NCRP's Plan are
designed to complement the changes to Social Security. The Commission outlined
changes in tax laws that would help more Americans to obtain private pension
coverage. The NCRP's Plan would reduce pension regulation and allow workers to
retain their pension assets more easily when they changed jobs. The Plan also
would increase personal retirement savings by expanding and simplifying
individual retirement accounts (IRAs), making tax-advantaged IRAs available to
all Americans.

A key element of the Commission's Plan—and potentially the most politically
difficult to enact—is a revised Social Security system. The compelling need for
reform of this vital program identified by the Commission dictates the need for
legislative action. It is precisely because of the nearly "sacrosanct" status of Social
Security, however, that politicians have proceeded so cautiously down the reform
path for fear of alienating voters—nearly all of whom have a vested interest in the
program. Both Republicans and Democrats are leery of embarking unilaterally on
reform measures for fear that their efforts will be used against them in the next
election cycle.

Those who, for policy or political reasons, oppose fundamental Social Security
reform legislation have an inherent advantage; a system in place is difficult to alter.

This is especially true if that system is viewed as a success. The politics of fear and labels of "radical" change can be exploited easily to place roadblocks in the way of reform. But it is precisely because Social Security is so important to Americans that efforts to save the system from insolvency should transcend party politics.

Leadership and statesmanship are the prerequisites for the ultimate success of any such effort. The Commission's Plan can serve as a framework for policymakers by demonstrating that bipartisan consensus for comprehensive detailed reform, not simply agreement on basic concepts, is possible when carried out in a deliberative, objective fashion.

The 21st Century Retirement Security Plan

Introduction

As the United States and its approximately 270 million citizens prepare for the beginning of the twenty-first century, we confront one of our greatest challenges as a country. The imminent retirement of the baby boom generation soon after the turn of the century will strain the fiscal capacity of the United States to ensure an adequate standard of living for those Americans moving into their golden years. Like other challenges our country has met, we will overcome this one too. Willpower alone will not be enough, however. This challenge will require Americans to reevaluate the financial partnership of government, employers, and individuals in providing retirement income for all citizens. It will take overt action by individuals and policymakers to recognize the issues we face and change our behavior and policies to prepare for the challenge. The initial step toward meeting the challenge successfully is acknowledging the situation. The first section of this report describes this looming problem.

Retirement Security in the Twenty-first Century

Quite simply, we as a country and as individuals are ill-prepared to meet the financial challenges of the twenty-first century. We are confronted with a rapidly aging population, actuarially unsound federal health and retirement programs, unsustainable trends of spending for government programs for senior citizens, and inadequate levels of private savings. We have promised too much and set aside too little. As a result, the proverbial "three-legged stool" of resources for retirement security—Social Security, personal savings, and private pension plans—that traditionally has financed Americans' retirement is becoming increasingly unstable and in need of repair.

Americans Know There Is a Problem

The problem is not one of abstract budgetary significance. Americans are anxious about their retirement, even at a time in which they are buoyed by high consumer confidence and the lowest level of unemployment in decades. Less than one in four Americans is "very confident" about being able to provide himself with a comfortable retirement.[2] The issue that causes the most insecurity for the average

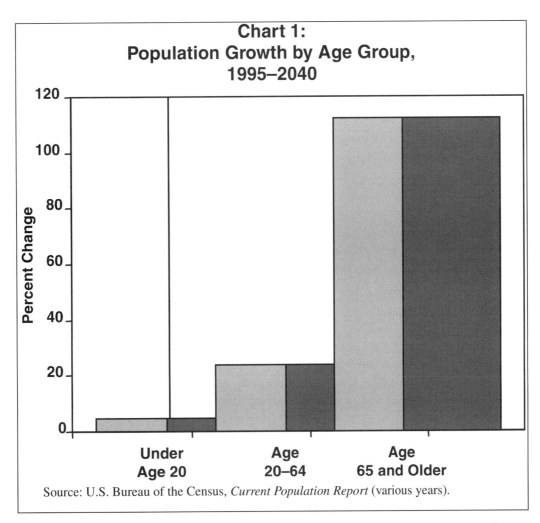

**Chart 1:
Population Growth by Age Group,
1995–2040**

Source: U.S. Bureau of the Census, *Current Population Report* (various years).

American is the uncertainty as to whether he will be able to retire in comfort.[3] Not only are Americans concerned that their own financial resources will be inadequate to provide for their retirement needs,[4] they no longer have confidence that the federal safety net—which has helped many seniors to avoid poverty—will be there to support them when they retire.[5]

For the past half century, a secure retirement has been part of the American dream. Now, however, as a result of immutable demographic changes, unsustainable fiscal trends, imprudent governmental policies, and individual choices, this dream may elude many Americans—or become an untenable economic burden on the next generation.

2. Paul Yakoboski and Pamela Ostuw, "What Is Your Savings Personality? The 1998 Retirement Confidence Survey," Employee Benefits Research Institute (EBRI) *Issue Brief* No. 200, August 1998, p. 7.

3. *USA Today* poll, October 26, 1996.

4. "Confronting the Savings Crisis: Perceptions and Attitudes About Retirement and Financial Planning," *Seventh Annual Merrill Lynch Retirement Planning Survey,* 1995, p. 2.

5. *Ibid.,* pp. 2, 4.

Americans Are Getting Older

Simply put, America is growing older. The aging of America has immense implications—both economic and social—for the country as a whole and for individuals.

The baby boom generation (the cohort born between 1946 and 1964) has exerted a profound effect on the United States at every stage of its collective development because of its massive size. The retirement of the baby boomers will prove no different.

Unfortunately, the baby boomers threaten to overwhelm the social insurance programs—Social Security and Medicare—as they presently are structured. These programs have thrived when funded by a growing number of working Americans, but they are not expected to have the necessary resources to meet future obligations unless corrective action is taken. For example:

❏ This year 200,000 Americans will turn 65 years old. In just 15 years, 1.6 million will be at least this age.[6]

❏ In 1900, 1 in 25 Americans was older than 65 years of age. Today, 1 in 8 Americans is 65 or older. By 2030, this percentage will increase to more than 20 percent, or 1 in 5. As a point of reference, the percentage of people over the age of 65 in Florida today is 18.4 percent; so, by 2030, the entire country will have similar demographics to Florida.[7] By 2040, nearly 1 in 4 will be 65 or older.[8]

❏ Today, there are approximately 24 million Americans over the age of 70. By 2030, the number will double to 48 million.[9]

Americans Are Living Longer but Not Necessarily Working Longer

As the large baby boom generation moves into retirement, one other complicating demographic factor arises: Americans are living longer.

❏ When Otto Von Bismarck created the first public pension system in Germany in 1891, the age for collecting benefits was set at 65 but the average life expectancy was just 45. When Social Security was created, the United States adopted 65 as the age at which one could receive full benefits. The average life expectancy at that time was 61 years, but today it is

---

6.   U.S. Department of Commerce, Bureau of the Census, "Sixty-Five Plus in the U.S.," at *http://www.census.gov*, May 1995, p. 1.

7.   U.S. Department of Commerce, Bureau of the Census, "Population Projections of the United States, by Age, Sex, Race, and Hispanic Origin, 1993–2050," *Current Population Report* No. P25–1104 (Washington, D.C.: U.S. Government Printing Office, 1993), Table 2.

8.   *Ibid.*

9.   Bipartisan Commission on Entitlement and Tax Reform, *Final Report to the President* (Washington, D.C.: U.S. Government Printing Office, 1995), p. 13.

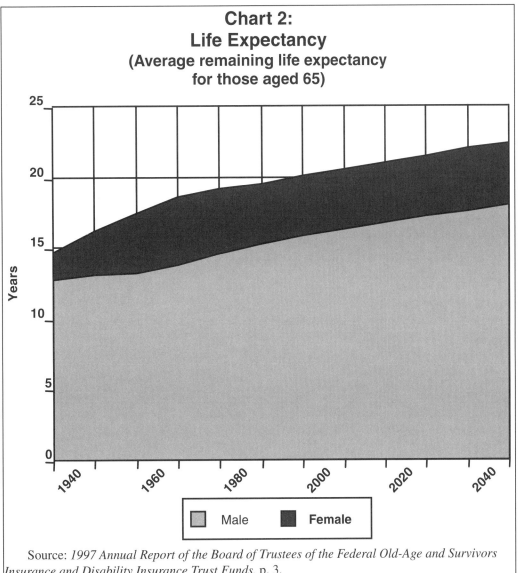

Chart 2:
Life Expectancy
(Average remaining life expectancy
for those aged 65)

Years

Male   Female

Source: *1997 Annual Report of the Board of Trustees of the Federal Old-Age and Survivors Insurance and Disability Insurance Trust Funds,* p. 3.

approximately 76; by the year 2025, it is expected to rise to 78.[10]

❏ At age 65 years, men are expected to live another 15 years, and women nearly 20 more years.[11]

❏ One in three baby girls born today is expected to reach nearly 90 years of age.[12]

10. Social Security Administration, *1997 Annual Report of the Board of Trustees of the Federal Old-Age and Survivors Insurance and Disability Insurance Trust Funds* (Washington, D.C.: U.S. Government Printing Office, 1997), p. 63.

11. *Ibid.*

12. Based on Annual Statistical Supplement, *Social Security Bulletin 1998,* p. 182, and intermediate data products used in the production of Social Security Administration, *1998 Annual Report of the Board of Trustees of the Federal Old-Age and Survivors Insurance and Disability Insurance Trust Funds* (Washington, D.C.: U.S. Government Printing Office, 1998).

> *We owe it to those who will retire after the turn of the century to be given sufficient advance notice to make what alterations in retirement planning may be required. The longer we wait to make what are surely inevitable adjustments, the more difficult they will become.*
> —Alan Greenspan, chairman of the Federal Reserve Board

Even as Americans live longer, they have been retiring earlier. In 1965, 57 percent of the population aged 55–65 was in the workforce. Today, that figure has dropped to 38 percent. Further, more than 70 percent of Social Security beneficiaries retire early, that is, before age 65.[13] As a result of these shifts, the average American will spend one-third of his adult life in retirement. The proverbial "golden years" of retirement are becoming the "golden *decades*." Those who instituted our federal safety net programs did not contemplate these significant changes over time.

Fewer Workers Will Be Available to Support the Growing Number of Retirees

A final complicating factor is the "baby bust" generation—the relatively small generation that follows the baby boomers. The average family had three children during the boom years (1946–1964), but that number decreased to less than two children from 1970 to 1990.[14] This has led to the marked decrease in the ratio of workers to Social Security beneficiaries. In 1950, there were 16.5 workers per beneficiary, but today there are merely 3.3 workers to support each beneficiary. By 2030, the ratio is expected to drop even further, to 2 workers supporting each beneficiary.[15] With productive capacity shrinking as the traditional labor force declines, only exceptional growth in productivity could ensure sufficient resources to sustain rising standards of living for aged and working Americans alike.

What Do These Trends Mean for Social Security?

Because Social Security is funded via intergenerational transfers, the lower fertility rates of the baby busters and the increasing longevity of the baby boomers have combined to erode the long-term solvency of the Social Security program.[16] Even though the financing problem is not immediate, there is widespread agreement that

---

13. Based on the OASDI's "Table of Numbers and Average Amount of Retired-Worker Benefits in Current Payments Status with and without Reduction for Early Retirement, by Sex, 1993–1997," at *http://www.tp.ssa.gov/pub/statistics/ic3*.

14. Based on "Table of Selected Demographic Assumptions by Alternative," Social Security Administration, *1997 Annual Report of the Board of Trustees of the Federal Old-Age and Survivors Insurance and Disability Insurance Trust Funds*, p. 63.

15. Based on "Table of Comparison of OASDI-Covered Workers and Beneficiaries by Alternative Years," Social Security Administration, *1997 Annual Report of the Board of Trustees of the Federal Old-Age and Survivors Insurance and Disability Insurance Trust Funds*, p. 124.

> *It is important to address the financing of both the OASDI and DI programs soon to allow time for phasing in any necessary changes and for workers to adjust their retirement plans to take account of those changes. The impact of the changes in the current program will be minimized if they are enacted soon.*
> —From the *1998 OASDI Trustees Report* (Highlights section)

the financial problem should be addressed soon if savings are to mitigate the impact of whatever reductions in benefits are chosen.

Beginning in 2008, the first baby boomers will reach 62, the age at which they become eligible for early retirement benefits. In its most recent report, the Social Security Board of Trustees tells us that shortly thereafter, Social Security will begin to experience an annual operating deficit.[17] This is true even though the current annual Trust Fund surplus is approximately $100 billion (including interest).[18]

The system then will begin to draw down its massive Trust Fund, which will have been accumulating principal and interest for decades. According to the trustees, the annual shortfalls will be bridged by Trust Fund interest alone until 2021. By that time, the majority of baby boomers will have retired and annual operating deficits will have soared to the point at which all interest is exhausted, and the system will begin to draw down Trust Fund principal. In 2032—despite all the years of surpluses—the Trust Fund will be exhausted, and revenue paid into the system at that time is expected to meet only approximately three-quarters of promised benefits. Accordingly, even though the Trust Fund will not become "insolvent" for just over three decades as defined under government accounting rules, this scenario nevertheless assumes that higher taxes will be imposed on future generations.

Insolvency versus Operating Shortfall

Moreover, reliance on the Trust Fund is misplaced. The massive account into which the annual operating surpluses are ostensibly deposited exists largely as a budgetary artifice instead of as a pool of actual assets. About one-half the Trust Fund surplus reflects the excess flow of payroll taxes over annual outlays to current beneficiaries. Under current law, Social Security surpluses can be invested only in federal treasury obligations that are credited to the Trust Fund. The government uses the money it borrows from the Trust Fund to meet current operating expenses or pay down national debt. The accumulated interest on these

---

16. The federal disability insurance program, referred to as DI, is in worse financial shape than the OASI Trust Fund. The Commission, however, did not address the issues raised by the federal disability insurance program.

17. Social Security Administration, *1998 Annual Report of the Board of Trustees of the Federal Old-Age and Survivors Insurance and Disability Insurance Trust Funds,* Highlights, April 1998, at *http://www.ssa.gov/OACT/TR/TR98.*

18. *Ibid.,* Table II.F.3.

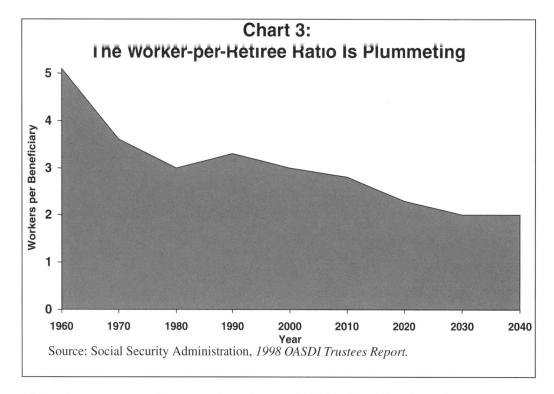

**Chart 3:
The Worker-per-Retiree Ratio Is Plummeting**

Source: Social Security Administration, *1998 OASDI Trustees Report.*

obligations accounts for approximately one-half the Trust Fund surplus.

Although, *in theory,* there is a Social Security Trust Fund that is accumulating large interest payments, *in reality,* the Trust Fund simply represents IOUs from one part of the government to another.[19]

The painful payback begins in 2013, when the Social Security system starts to take in less revenue than it pays out in benefits. At that point, the federal government will have to face two very unpleasant realities. First, the absence of cash flow into the Trust Fund will deprive the government of a source of revenue it has used to meet current operating expenses. Second, and perhaps more important, starting in 2013 the government will have to find the money to pay off its debt to the Social Security system. The annual shortfalls will increase rapidly thereafter, from an estimated $49 billion in 2015 to $684 billion in 2030.[20] Even though a large amount theoretically will remain of the Social Security Trust Fund, the federal government will either have to squeeze all non–Social Security parts of the government in order to service the obligations of the Social Security system, raise taxes, borrow from the public, or reduce the promised benefits.

---

19. It should be noted that these federal obligations have the full faith and credit of the federal government behind them. The fiscal concern, as discussed later in this report, is the manner in which the government obtains the resources to meet the massive obligations.

20. Social Security Administration, *1998 Annual Report of the Board of Trustees of the Federal Old-Age and Survivors Insurance and Disability Insurance Trust Funds,* Table III-B4, excluding interest, p. 181.

Table 1: Financial Status of Social Security[a]

Year	Income (Excluding Interest)	Outgo	Surplus/ Deficit
	($ in billions, 1998 intermediate projection of Social Security Trustees)		
1998	435	383	52
1999	450	396	54
2000	468	413	54
2005	585	533	52
2010	756	724	32
2015	965	1,014	-49
2020	1,217	1,430	-214
2025	1,525	1,958	-433
2030	1,917	2,601	-684
2035	2,418	3,342	-925
2040	3,043	4,190	-1,147

a. Source: *1998 Board of Trustees Report,* Office of the Chief Actuary, Social Security Administration, Table III–B-4.

Payroll Tax Increases Are Not the Answer

While funding gaps can be bridged by raising payroll taxes, this would impose a substantial burden on many American families. Indeed, nearly 80 percent of families pay more in payroll taxes (Social Security and Medicare combined) than in income taxes.[21]

Although a payroll tax hike of 2 percent imposed immediately on all working Americans would, in theory, address Social Security's long-term actuarial deficiency by beefing up the current Social Security surplus, it would do little to alleviate the tremendous cash flow problems that arise when all the baby boomers are in retirement. Moreover, this would only exacerbate the tendency of the federal government to spend the Social Security surplus on other programs.

Public support for payroll tax increases would have its limits as the concern of today's workers grew with regard to the rate of return the present system yields on their significant lifetime contributions to Social Security in the form of payroll taxes. In order to provide the current level of benefits, Social Security payroll taxes have risen since the inception of the program from 2 percent to 12.4 percent, and

21. Combined employee and employer portions of payroll taxes; figures for 1995 from "Estimates of Federal Tax Liabilities For Individuals and Families by Income Category and Family Type for 1995 and 1999," Congressional Budget Office (Washington, D.C.: U.S. Government Printing Office, May 1998), p. 5.

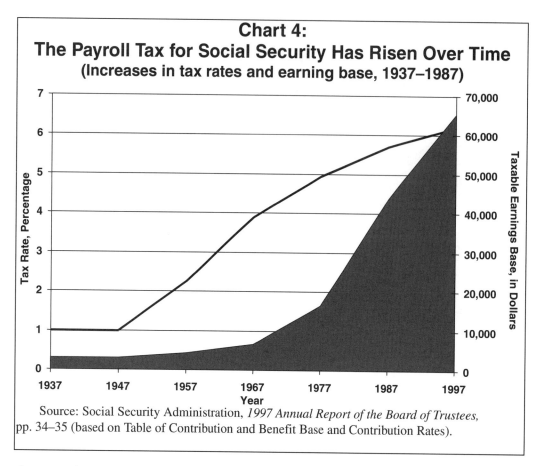

Chart 4:
The Payroll Tax for Social Security Has Risen Over Time
(Increases in tax rates and earning base, 1937–1987)

Source: Social Security Administration, *1997 Annual Report of the Board of Trustees,* pp. 34–35 (based on Table of Contribution and Benefit Base and Contribution Rates).

the wage base (that is, the income limit up to which one is taxed) from $3,000 to $68,400.[22] In the view of the Commission, these "traditional" solutions to financial shortfalls also have proved only temporary in nature, due to the fact that they treat a symptom of the problem rather than remedying faults in the design of the underlying system that continually lead to the funding shortfalls. For those reasons, the Commission chose programmatic reforms, as opposed to increased taxes, to stave off the Social Security system's insolvency. For a detailed summary of the Commission's recommendations on Social Security reforms, see Appendix A.

Public Pension Solvency Is Only One Ingredient

Even as policymakers devise a plan to ensure the future solvency of the Social Security Trust Fund, they know their job is not done. Studies reveal that Social Security forms the bulk of retirement income for the majority of retired Americans. Social Security benefits provide the major source of income for *66 percent* of beneficiaries—and the *only* source of income for 18 percent.[23] Considering that the maximum Social Security benefit paid this year is $1,342 per

22. Dave Koitz, "New Benefit Awards as a Percentage of Final Year's Earnings," Social Security: Brief Facts and Statistics, Congressional Research Service (CRS) *Report for Congress* No. 94–27 EPW, updated May 1998, pp. 4 and 5.

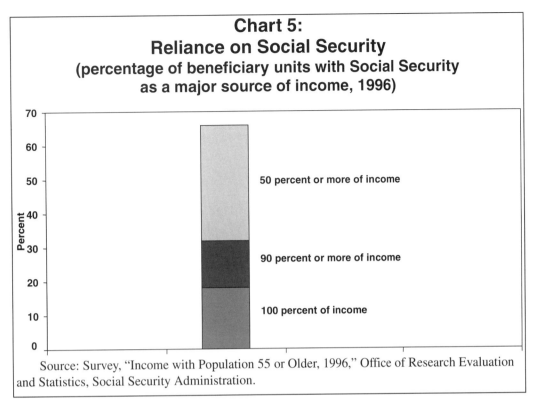

**Chart 5:
Reliance on Social Security**
(percentage of beneficiary units with Social Security
as a major source of income, 1996)

Source: Survey, "Income with Population 55 or Older, 1996," Office of Research Evaluation and Statistics, Social Security Administration.

month, and that the benefit for a person who earned an average salary is $938 per month,[24] more needs to be done to help to ensure adequate retirement for all Americans. Social Security benefits were intended only to provide an income "floor" for beneficiaries. In other words, retirement security requires that public pensions be supplemented by individual savings and private pension benefits. The average monthly Social Security benefit for a retired worker in July 1998 was $767,[25] less than the gross monthly salary from a minimum wage job.[26]

Nor can the federal government continue to spend increasing amounts of money on "automatic spending" programs without consequence.

Mandatory spending and interest on the national debt account for nearly two-thirds of current federal spending, according to the Congressional Budget Office (CBO).[27] The President's Bipartisan Commission on Entitlement and Tax Reform in 1994 found that, without changes, entitlement programs will consume all federal revenues by 2030—and, if interest on the national debt is included in the

---

23. Age 65 and older (1996), Social Security Administration Office of Research, Evaluation, and Statistics, *Fast Facts and Figures About Social Security 1998,* p. 7.

24. Social Security Administration Web site, *http://www.ssa.gov,* Budget and Planning, Actuarial Information, Benefit Amounts for Hypothetical Cases.

25. Social Security Administration Web site, *http://www.ssa.gov,* Highlights of Social Security Data, July 1998.

26. Assuming 160 work hours per month (four weeks/40 hours) at current federal minimum wage of $5.15 per hour. There is a difference between the benefit of a worker earning the national average income and the average benefit paid by Social Security. The average Social Security benefit takes into account survivor's benefits, those with very low earnings histories, and so forth.

27. Based on Congressional Budget Office, "Table of the Budget Outlook through 1997," *Economic and Budget Outlook* (Washington, D.C.: U.S. Government Printing Office), p. xii.

calculations, this date accelerates to 2018.[28] The Balanced Budget Act of 1997[29] and a strong economy have improved the short term outlook. But the trend remains unsustainable. And, even though the CBO recently predicted additional federal government surpluses, it underscored that when the baby boomers begin to retire, annual deficits will return and grow increasingly larger thereafter, due primarily to growth in entitlement expenditures on the elderly.[30]

The current unfunded liability of Social Security through 2070 is estimated to be $5.3 trillion.[31] Under present law, benefits under Social Security and Medicare combined will exceed current projected payroll tax revenues by nearly $19 trillion between 1997 and 2070.[32]

Although additional government resources can, and undoubtedly will, be diverted to meet a significant portion of the obligation, such expenditure does not come without a cost. Resources dedicated to old-age benefits will be unavailable for welfare programs, education, investments in infrastructure, national defense, or other government programs. This potential "squeezing out" of other priorities was of particular concern to Commission members and a principal reason for moving toward a partially prefunded Social Security system.

An Increased Role for Individual Responsibility

Because policymakers have overpromised when it comes to the future benefits of the system, debate about Social Security will take center stage in the 106th Congress. Increasingly, Americans are coming to the realization that they will have to assume greater responsibility for a secure retirement instead of relying on the limited resources of the government.

According to one public opinion poll, only 13 percent of workers expect Social Security to provide the largest portion of their retirement income. Furthermore, 21 percent of workers do not expect any retirement income from Social Security.[33] Many Americans understand the need to plan for their own retirement. Unfortunately, however, the realization that one needs to accumulate personal assets for retirement does not always translate into action.

Social Security benefits today, on average, replace approximately 42 percent of preretirement income for beneficiaries, a share that will fall to 34 percent in 2030.[34] Financial planners suggest that most people would need between 60 percent and 80 percent of preretirement earnings to maintain their same standard of living in

---

28. Based on figures from the Congressional Budget Office, "Long-Term Budget Outlook," March 1997, p. xv.

29. H.R. 2015, P.L. 105–33.

30. Congressional Budget Office, "Long-Term Budgetary Pressures and Policy Options," Summary, May 1998, p. 1.

31. OASDI, *1997 Annual Report of the Board of Trustees,* p. 184.

32. *Ibid.*

33. Yakoboski and Ostuw, "What Is Your Savings Personality? The 1998 Retirement Confidence Survey," p. 8.

34. New retiree age 65 in 1998. From Koitz, "New Benefit Awards as a Percentage of Final Year's Earnings," p. 10.

retirement. Even if Social Security were able to maintain the current level of retirement income for future beneficiaries, private pensions and savings would have quite a gap to fill.

Employer-sponsored Pensions

Many private- and public-sector employers offer their workers a pension plan, either a defined-benefit plan (in which benefits are calculated by a formula and are based typically on pay, years of service, and other factors) or a defined-contribution plan, such as a 401(k) plan (in which specified contributions are made to participant's individual accounts, coming from either, or both, the employer or employee).

Pensions can be an important source of retirement income. In the past 20 years, the aggregate percentage of retirement income derived from private pensions has grown from 16 percent to 30 percent,[35] but many workers do not participate in or have access to such plans.

❏ Fewer than 50 percent of workers participate in an employer-sponsored pension plan at any given time.[36]

❏ Fewer than 30 percent of low-income workers participate in an employer-sponsored pension plan.[37]

❏ Only about 30 percent of employees of small businesses (businesses with 100 or fewer employees) are covered by a pension plan at work, and, of these, and only 21 percent participate. This means that only about 10 million out of the approximately 35 million employees of small businesses have access to a retirement plan at their job, and that only about 7 million of them actually participate.[38]

❏ Even though pension coverage at large businesses is much better—83 percent of employees are covered by pension plans—only 64 percent of those eligible actually choose to participate in the plans.[39]

❏ Even those who do participate in an employer-provided pension plan often fail to take full advantage of the benefit. For example, of those contributing to 401(k) defined-contribution plans, only 21 percent put in the maximum amount that their employer would match.[40]

35. Based on EBRI, "Table of Total Retirement Benefit Payments," *Retirement Prospects in a Defined Contribution World,* April 30, 1997.

36. "Employment-Based Retirement Income Benefits: Analysis of the April 1993 Current Population Survey," EBRI *Special Report,* September 1994, p. 1.

37. Based on Carolyn Pemberton and Deborah Holmes, eds., "Table of Retirement Plan Sponsorship, Participation, and Vesting, 1993," *Databook on Employee Benefits,* 3rd ed. (Washington, D.C.: EBRI, 1996), p. 73.

38. From EBRI and American Savings Education Council, "Small Business Employer Retirement Survey," press release, June 2, 1998.

39. *Ibid.*

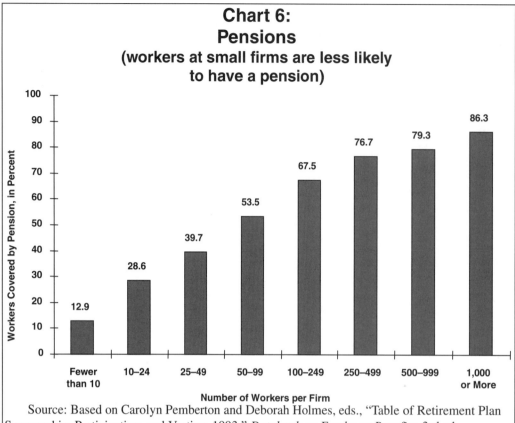

Chart 6:
Pensions
(workers at small firms are less likely to have a pension)

Source: Based on Carolyn Pemberton and Deborah Holmes, eds., "Table of Retirement Plan Sponsorship, Participation, and Vesting, 1993," *Databook on Employee Benefits,* 3rd ed. (Washington, D.C.: EBRI, 1996), p. 73.

The Leakage of Retirement Savings

An additional problem with pension plans is that many who do participate end up withdrawing a significant portion of the assets prior to retirement. Specifically, one of every four participants intends to use pension savings for making a downpayment on a house or paying for a child's education.[41] In 1996, only 40 percent of all distributions from defined-contribution plans made to people changing jobs were rolled over into other tax-deferred retirement plans.[42] The statistics become even worse for accounts with fewer assets: only 20 percent of distributions of less then $3,500 were rolled over into tax-deferred retirement accounts.[43]

More often than not, those retirement assets not rolled over are simply spent. Thus, the worker not only has lost assets, he also has squandered valuable time needed for financial assets to grow through "compounding." The preservation of

---

40. "The Reality of Retirement Today: Lessons in Planning for Tomorrow," EBRI *Issue Brief,* January 1997, p. 8.

41. Marshall Carter, "Trends in World Financial Markets," speech to the Boston Economic Club, April 5, 1995, p. 9.

42. Paul Yakoboski, "Large Lump-Sum Rollovers and Cashouts," EBRI *Issue Brief* No. 188, August 1997, p. 7.

43. *Ibid.*

even a modest amount of retirement plan distributions over time can grow to considerable sums over the course of a full career.

The changing nature of the labor force also affects the accumulation of pension assets. Today, it is not unusual for a worker to have several employers throughout his career. Workers changing jobs cannot always take their pensions with them. Different types of pension plans and differing regulatory rules can limit the "portability" of assets from one employer's plan to another. The inability to transfer pension assets freely could yield a lower retirement income than if the worker had been able to move those assets independently from one plan to the next as easily as he had changed jobs. Moreover, pension assets can be lost if there is no portability, resulting in increasing issues associated with "missing participants" who cannot be found due to job and address changes. The NCRP was concerned that the lack of portability, coupled with "leakage," has such a significant adverse effect on the accumulation of retirement assets.

Despite improvements over the past decade, vast room for improvement remains in pension participation, both on the part of the employer in making plans available, and on the part of the employee in taking full advantage of such plans.

For the millions of Americans who do not have a retirement savings vehicle available to them through their employers, accumulating financial resources for retirement will depend on personal savings habits.

Personal Savings

Individual savings accumulated during working years can help to ensure a financially secure retirement. This is especially necessary, as highlighted above, for those individuals who do not participate in a pension plan and rely disproportionately on Social Security benefits as their means of a modest floor of income protection.

Evidence indicates that Americans have become increasingly aware of the importance of personal savings (for example, IRAs, stocks, bonds, bank accounts, and personal assets including home equity) for retirement security, having been bombarded by mountains of data and studies appearing in the media and through both public and private institutions. This educational effort is having a positive effect. A recent poll reveals that nearly two-thirds (63 percent) of Americans personally had saved money for retirement at some point in 1998.[44] Although the fact that the majority of Americans are saving is a very positive trend, it still means that over one-third is not saving for retirement at all. Furthermore, many of those who are saving apparently are not putting away anything close to the amounts necessary to ensure an adequate retirement. In 1998, the personal savings rate for Americans was a scant 3.9 percent of disposable income, approaching the savings lows of the Great Depression.[45] (In the last quarter of the year, the rate actually was

44. Yakoboski and Ostuw, "What Is Your Savings Personality? The 1998 Retirement Confidence Survey," p. 9.

45. Savings as a percentage of disposable income. *Source:* U. S. Department of Commerce, Bureau of Economic Analysis.

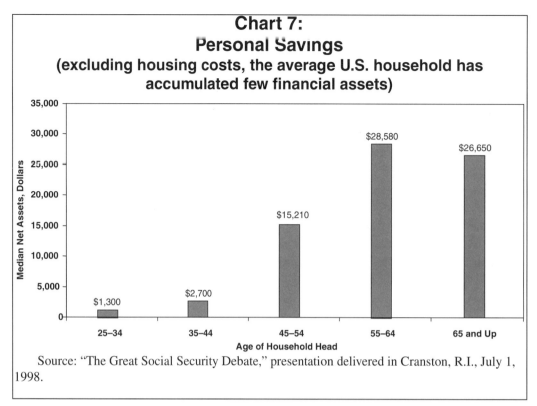

**Chart 7:
Personal Savings
(excluding housing costs, the average U.S. household has
accumulated few financial assets)**

Source: "The Great Social Security Debate," presentation delivered in Cranston, R.I., July 1, 1998.

negative.) By contrast, in 1981 the personal savings rate was 9.1 percent of income.[46] This precipitous drop in the rate of saving, concludes one study, means that families are saving at only about one-third the rate necessary to replicate their present standard of living in retirement.[47]

One indication of the attitude of Americans toward savings is their use of IRAs. In 1992, the most recent year for which figures are available, only 10 percent of eligible taxpayer households made *tax-deductible* contributions to IRAs, even though two-thirds of American households were eligible.[48] If Americans are not taking greater advantage of a savings instrument that actually can lower their taxes, it is unlikely that they are taking advantage of other significant retirement savings.

It is little wonder, then, that a recent survey shows that only 24 percent of workers say they are "very confident" about being able to provide themselves with a comfortable retirement.[49]

One explanation for such a lack of collective confidence is that increased awareness of retirement needs can lead to intimidation and discouragement. A vital first step toward preparing for retirement is to estimate as accurately as

46. *Ibid.*

47. Does not include housing wealth. From a study conducted by B. Douglas Bernheim of Stanford University, cited in Jonathan Weisman, "Rainy Days Get No Respect as Savings Rate Droops," *Congressional Quarterly,* January 17, 1998, p. 116.

48. Paul Yakoboski, "IRA Eligibility and Usage," EBRI *Notes,* Vol. 16, No. 4 (April 1995), p. 6.

49. Yakoboski and Ostuw, "What Is Your Savings Personality? The 1998 Retirement Confidence Survey," p. 7.

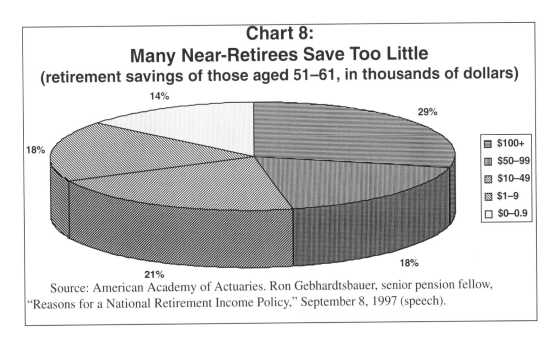

Chart 8:
Many Near-Retirees Save Too Little
(retirement savings of those aged 51–61, in thousands of dollars)

Legend:
- $100+
- $50–99
- $10–49
- $1–9
- $0–0.9

14%
29%
18%
18%
21%

Source: American Academy of Actuaries. Ron Gebhardtsbauer, senior pension fellow, "Reasons for a National Retirement Income Policy," September 8, 1997 (speech).

possible how much money one will need. Often, the resulting estimated gross figures in these calculations are staggering, in the *hundreds of thousands* of dollars for even those of relatively modest income whose goal is only to maintain their present lifestyle in retirement. Such information can be a powerful motivator for action with some, but can be daunting to others who may conclude that it is useless even to try to attain such sums.

Even among those who are *not* presently saving, however, the clear majority (55 percent) admit that it is reasonably possible to save $20 a week for retirement.[50] In today's world, $20 each week involves only very modest changes in one's present behavior, perhaps as simple as not buying that gourmet cup of coffee every day or bringing lunch to work from home two or three days a week. Saving that modest amount of money consistently over a working career, however, could have a huge impact on one's lifestyle in retirement.

Although the estimated needs for retirement figures can be intimidating, the power of compounding over a long period of time can be equally staggering. For example, if a 25-year-old started saving that $20 per week and continued to do so until he retired at age 65, assuming a very modest rate of return of 5 percent, his nest egg would be nearly $132,000.[51]

It is critically important to start saving early; time is the key to the power of compounding. For example, if a 25-year-old person began saving $50 each week until he reached age 65 (assuming a return of 5 percent on those savings), he would have amassed approximately $302,305. If that same person waited until age 35 to start saving the same $50, however—assuming the same rate of return—his total at age 65 would be approximately half ($165,130) of what he would have by starting to save just 10 years earlier.[52]

---

50. *Ibid.*, p. 11.
51. *Ibid.*

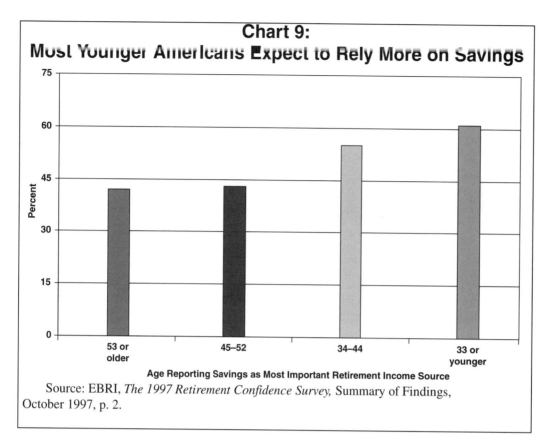

Chart 9:
Most Younger Americans Expect to Rely More on Savings

Age Reporting Savings as Most Important Retirement Income Source

Source: EBRI, *The 1997 Retirement Confidence Survey,* Summary of Findings, October 1997, p. 2.

The fact that many Americans fail to build adequate retirement savings is not for lack of available tools. The trick is getting people to utilize those instruments to their fullest advantage. The challenge for government lies in providing the proper level of incentives to bolster personal savings and, at a minimum, not enacting policies that make it more difficult for employers and individuals to establish retirement savings plans. Increased private rates of saving, of course, will relieve some of the pressure on public assistance: the more Americans save personally and through their employer pension plans, the more capital will become available to grow the economy, which, in turn, will provide the government with more power to ensure the stability of the Social Security system. The more Americans save personally, the more secure their personal retirements. This comprehensive view of retirement security was the cornerstone of the NCRP's ideology and precipitated the comprehensive approach to retirement savings described below.

A Comprehensive Plan Proposed

The Commission undertook to design a plan that would improve each of the three legs of retirement savings.

The result of the Commission's 18-month effort is the 21st Century Retirement Security Plan (the Plan), which the Commission's members adopted *unanimously.*

---

52. American Savings Education Council, *401(k) Growth Calculator* (Boston, Mass.: Advantage Publications, 1995).

Why Did CSIS Establish a National Commission on Retirement Policy?

As discussed in the preceding sections, laying the foundation for economic growth and prosperity in the face of the profound demographic changes that will occur early in the next century is, perhaps, the most difficult challenge facing our country. The imminent retirement of the baby boom generation, combined with longer life expectancies and poor fiscal discipline, will place extraordinary pressure on the fabric of the federal safety net programs and could imperil the standard of living of future generations. Unless Americans save more and spend less, our country will be confronted with a Hobson's choice: dramatically lower standards of living for current retirees or an untenable tax burden on future retirees.

CSIS established the National Commission on Retirement Policy to respond to these challenges. Created in January 1997, the 24-member commission was composed of leaders from the public and private sectors and included policymakers, economists, and experts on retirement savings. These leaders came together to deliberate the facts and design a proposal to meet the challenge of ensuring a financially secure retirement for all Americans as well as to place the country on a path toward long-term economic security.

The NCRP believes that essential elements of a comprehensive plan to address retirement security in the twenty-first century must:

- reform Social Security to provide long-term solvency to the system;
- enhance the ability of employers to provide pensions and savings plans;
- stimulate growth in personal savings; and
- educate the public about the need to plan, save, and invest for retirement.

The NCRP established as its goal that a "broad-based, bipartisan national retirement policy should be developed and implemented as soon as practicable to respond to this [retirement security] challenge." The NCRP established this goal after adopting three guiding principles at the beginning of its deliberative process:

1. National retirement policy should be designed to enable Americans to enjoy a reasonable standard of living in their retirement years. It should encompass government programs that require a floor of financial support for elderly retirees as well as initiatives that encourage and facilitate group (that is, employer) and individual saving to provide additional retirement income above the floor of support.

2. National retirement policy should contribute to long-term growth and economic prosperity.

3. Government programs for elderly retirees should be financially sound and economically sustainable. The costs of financing these programs and other initiatives that encourage and facilitate national saving should be borne equitably.

In order to develop these elements, the NCRP embarked on an extensive examination of the problems the United States and its citizens face with respect to future retirement and a deliberative debate on suggested solutions.

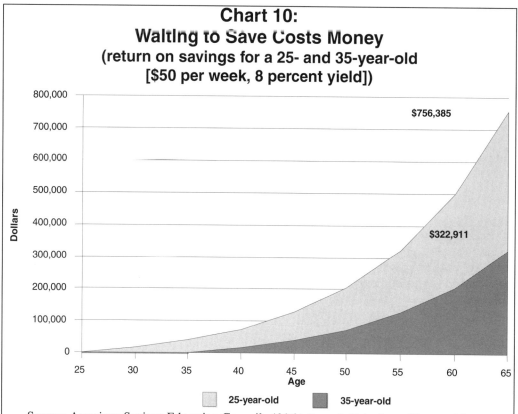

**Chart 10:
Waiting to Save Costs Money
(return on savings for a 25- and 35-year-old
[$50 per week, 8 percent yield])**

Source: American Savings Education Council, *401(k) Growth Calculator* (Boston, Mass.: Advantage Publications). Note: The advantage of saving earlier is offset somewhat by the effect of inflation; the opportunity cost of saving is greater in the earliest 10 years than it is later. The benefits of compounding, however, more than make up the difference.

The Plan is unique in its comprehensive bipartisan approach for repairing and improving all three major sources of retirement income. It reflects substantive policy changes in both the public and private savings areas.

At the heart of the Plan is a commitment to enhance retirement security for all Americans, especially those most in need. The Plan is grounded in a basic faith in, and optimism about, the future of our country, the economy, and the American people. The Plan would allow individuals to harness for themselves a piece of the power and growth potential that has driven our country to its preeminence—the free-market system—to the end of improving the fate both of the individual and of the country. The Plan also would allow the individual to take an active part in the investment of a portion of his Social Security payroll taxes while maintaining a modified guaranteed benefit. The key is that managed risk, in the context of the prolonged, strong U.S. economic climate and the luxury of time, has proved quite rewarding for both the United States and its citizens.

Although improvements conceivably could be made to individual elements of the Plan, the Commission believes that the complete package of reforms offers a unified national retirement policy that is fiscally responsible, practically achievable, and politically viable.

A Comprehensive Plan for a Complex Problem

The 21st Century Retirement Security Plan is unique in that it is a comprehensive approach to retirement security that incorporates a number of elements that work together to enhance retirement security for all Americans. The Plan is designed not only to restore Social Security to a sound financial footing, but also to expand pension coverage and enhance personal savings opportunities. Much like the diversification of investments to spread risk, the more evenly spread one's retirement assets are among Social Security, private pensions, and personal savings, the greater the chances for a successful, secure retirement.

Preserving Universal Social Security

Perhaps the most novel proposals in the Commission's Plan are the creation of ISAs, which would allow for individual investment of a portion of existing Social Security payroll taxes, and the establishment of a new Minimum Benefit Guarantee, which would protect the most vulnerable in our society from poverty. The Plan's two-tiered approach to Social Security reform—involving both a traditional defined benefit and individual accounts—would lessen the huge unfunded liability on future generations and offer the potential for improved benefits for all workers. The combined traditional Social Security benefit and ISA would improve retirement income by providing higher rates of return and replacement rates on preretirement income than the current system. The Commission's Plan also would strengthen basic safety through the establishment of a guaranteed minimum Social Security benefit, which would ensure that someone who worked throughout his life would receive at least a poverty-level Social Security benefit—a protection that does not exist under current law.

　　The Commission believes this approach offers several advantages. It would provide greater retirement income security for those most in need; it would evoke a sense of thrift among workers who had not invested previously; it should increase the national savings rate; and it would increase the return on the earnings of American workers. Although many legitimate issues remain as to how best to structure and administer individual accounts, the Commission believes policymakers should work through these issues to design a system that incorporates this component.

The Plan Would Enhance Private Savings

The Commission recognized that Social Security benefits alone, although presenting a modest floor of income protection, fall far short of providing for a secure retirement. Social Security benefits replace less than half of the preretirement income for the average-income worker. Clearly, supplemental retirement resources are an essential component for retired Americans to achieve adequate financial independence in their golden years.

Despite the demonstrated need, Americans as a whole fail to accumulate the assets necessary to provide for any meaningful income supplement to Social Security in retirement. Only about one-half the workforce participates in an employer-sponsored pension plan, and coverage reaches alarmingly low levels among small business, low-income, and minority workers. The tax code—despite some recent improvements—seems to have been written with an eye more focused on federal revenues than on encouraging personal savings. Not surprisingly, personal savings rates, even in this period of economic expansion, have reached Depression-era lows.

It is important to remember that pension coverage and personal savings are totally voluntary. Employers are not compelled by law to offer pension plans; nor are individuals required to save for their futures. The Commission believes that incentives should be enhanced and simplified so that these underutilized savings vehicles would become more effective tools for accumulating sufficient retirement assets. Therefore, although restoring the fiscal stability of Social Security is imperative for ensuring a floor of income for future retirees, the 21st Century Retirement Plan simultaneously would strengthen the other two legs of retirement income.

Higher Savings Are the Key to National Economic Growth

The benefits of higher savings affect us as individuals and as a country. Increased individual savings can have a direct correlation on economic growth by increasing the amount of investment capital available to businesses and lowering borrowing costs. Economic growth yields more revenue and a stronger economy so that the government will be better able to meet the financial obligations it has undertaken. The 21st Century Retirement Security Plan was designed to encourage savings and investment on the individual level, which, in turn, would generate an interplay of forces with positive macroeconomic ramifications on a national level.

Therefore, restoring the long-term solvency of the federal retirement systems, while absolutely essential, cannot represent the sole objective of any federal retirement plan aimed at ensuring that all Americans can retire with financial security. Policymakers must realize that changes imposed on the structure of Social Security can have a profound effect on the private pension structure and private savings needs. This is precisely the aim of the 21st Century Retirement Security Plan.

Strengthening the three traditional principal sources of retirement simultaneously would allow the American worker access to a variety of tools with which to build a secure retirement and, at the same time, would strengthen the U.S. economy by fostering a country of savers.

The fact that the NCRP debated these very issues and was able to reach a consensus is an encouraging sign as the debate moves toward concrete action in the halls of Congress and inside the Clinton administration. The 21st Century Retirement Security Plan is tangible evidence that a bipartisan group of policymakers can reach agreement on even the toughest and most emotional issues. The Commission hopes its Plan will serve our current elected leaders well as they undertake to save the Social Security program and shore up private savings in the United States. This is an important journey we, as Americans, will endeavor to take together. We hope the 21st Century Retirement Security Plan will help to map the rocky terrain that lies ahead.

The 21st Century Retirement Security Plan in Detail

This document provides a more detailed description of the 21st Century Retirement Security Plan. It describes the Commission's specific proposals to improve the current system, enhance private pension plans, and encourage personal savings. It also includes the underlying assumptions that the Commission used, discusses issues related to the administration of individual accounts, compares three additional NCRP reform plans, and provides an explanation of distributional effects.

Social Security: Detailed Description

Introduction to Detailed Description

The 21st Century Retirement Security Plan reflects the Commission's finding that the challenge facing Social Security is fundamentally demographic. Social Security has functioned efficiently and well for America's seniors during the periods in which working generations have been sufficiently numerous to provide for retirees on a pay-as-you-go basis.

The shape of the demographic curve that the United States will move through early in the next century makes advance funding desirable for Social Security in order to avoid unacceptable tax burdens on the economy of the twenty-first century. It also is imperative that the Social Security system offer strengthened rewards for work as an extra safeguard against declining worker–collector ratios.

This section describes in further detail the specific proposals in the Commission's Plan for strengthening the Social Security system. These proposals would modernize the Social Security system to allow individuals more personal choice and greater growth potential for their funds through the creation of ISAs, funded by payroll contributions. The Plan would keep Social Security solvent for the next 70 years without tax increases; improve benefits for lower-income workers; encourage seniors to continue working by allowing them to keep their earnings without reducing their benefits; and establish minimum benefits to help the most vulnerable. Provisions to shift ages of eligibility gradually upward reflect the necessity to limit the decline in the worker-to-collector ratio.

The detailed descriptions that follow set forth the details of these proposals and compare them with present law, where applicable, to explain the reasons the Commission included them in its Plan.

Social Security: Recommendations

Individual Security Accounts

Refund two percentage points of the current 12.4-percent payroll tax into individual accounts.

The 21st Century Retirement Security Plan would refund two percentage points of Social Security's current 12.4 percent Old-Age and Survivors Insurance and Disability Insurance (OASDI) program tax into ISAs. This feature is included for the following reasons, as well as for others:

1. Confining reforms to the traditional alternatives, such as increasing tax revenues or reducing benefit growth, would have adverse effects on the rate of return that individual beneficiaries, especially young workers, received from Social Security. Even though the rate of return is not the only criterion by which Social Security reforms should be evaluated, it is nevertheless an important means of measuring the intergenerational equity of the program as well as the enduring political support it is likely to enjoy.

2. The current structure of the system, in which Social Security's assets are invested in the aggregate in treasury securities alone, precludes advance funding because these securities are redeemed solely by general taxation. Thus, an unrestructured system mandates that the burden of funding tomorrow's retirement income benefits will fall exclusively on tomorrow's taxpayers. In order to fund some of the future benefits of Social Security directly, it would become necessary that a portion of these benefits be financed with other assets.

3. The Commission believes that most Americans would receive more retirement income from the Social Security program if ISAs were incorporated into the system than they would receive if traditional solutions alone were used to bring the system back into balance.

4. The Commission also believes that, even with conservative estimates of the rates of return, ISAs would not entail a significant increase in economic risk for beneficiaries when combined with the additional protections against poverty contained in the Plan.

5. The Commission is confident that the transition costs to such a system are manageable. Today, the OASDI system generates a surplus of sufficient size to permit two percentage points of the current payroll tax to be refunded into ISAs. Assets would continue to accumulate within the traditional Social Security Trust Fund, of which no principal need be redeemed in the short term in order to meet benefit promises to current beneficiaries. Furthermore, updated federal unified budget projections suggest that, by the time of the enactment of this Plan, it will be possible for the federal government to permit a payroll tax refund of 2 percent of payroll without incurring a federal deficit.

6. Because the near-term federal unified budget surplus is attributable to the annual operating surplus of the OASDI program, the Commission deemed it appropriate to use a portion of this latter surplus explicitly to fund in advance

the future liabilities of the Social Security system instead of going to underwrite the present-day operations of the federal government.

7. The Commission believed that requiring an additional contribution from individuals above the current 12.4 percent tax rate as governed by the Federal Insurance Contributions Act (FICA)—even though it could improve the rate of return that individuals received from Social Security—would be a less desirable means of establishing ISAs. The Commission believes that contributors would perceive an extra mandatory contribution as a tax increase that would absorb income that no longer would be available for other pressing needs, ranging from meeting Medicare costs to providing additional retirement income through employer-provided pensions and personal saving.

Although the Commission's Plan would not require additional contributions beyond the current 12.4 percent OASDI tax rate, individuals would be permitted to save up to an additional $2,000 per year (net of any IRA contributions) as an additional element of any Social Security ISA. This $2,000 limit would be indexed annually for inflation. Any voluntary contributions to an ISA would receive the same tax treatment as nondeductible IRA contributions under current law; that is, contributions would not be tax-deductible and only taxes on accumulated earnings would be deferred until distributed. Voluntary contributions to an ISA would be permitted one year after the implementation of the mandatory ISA feature, provided that it is administratively feasible to do so.

The Commission devoted several hearings and meetings to the question of designing and administering individual accounts. Inefficiency in the design and administration of this system would produce several undesirable results, ranging from administrative costs that were larger than projected investment returns for low-income workers to unwieldy new administrative burdens on small employers. The Commission concluded that the Thrift Savings Plan (TSP), the retirement savings plan of federal employees administered by the Office of Personnel Management, provides the best model for designing the personal account component in a way that does not introduce such difficulties. A further description of the Commission's recommendations on the administration and regulation of ISAs is included below.

In addition, the Commission supports requiring the Social Security Administration to provide information to individuals on their Social Security benefits (for example, defined-benefit accounts and ISA benefits) once per year either in electronic or print format. This information should include reasonable and understandable ways for participants to estimate the value of their benefits at retirement. The government should lead by example in connection with providing information to taxpayers on their individual retirement benefits. Any such disclosures should address both a person's base defined benefit and any ISA element. In addition, any projections should be based on reasonable and fully disclosed assumptions that are consistent with current law and the projected funding status of the Social Security program.

Increase Minimum Benefits

The Commission recommends a minimum benefit provision that individuals would be eligible for after 20 years of covered earnings. All Social Security beneficiaries with 20 years of covered earnings would be guaranteed a benefit of at least 60 percent of the poverty level, phasing upward at 2 percent with each year of covered earnings until it reaches 100 percent of the poverty level after 40 years of work. The minimum benefit provision would become fully effective in 2010.

This provision was included in each of the four plans developed by the Social Security Working Group. It reflects the view of the Commission that the progressivity of the traditional benefit structure within Social Security must be increased, especially if an ISA element is included, with which no progressive effect is assumed. This provision would shield low-income recipients from the adverse effects of other measures taken to restore the Social Security system to solvency. It also would ensure that individuals run no risk of being left in poverty despite a lifetime of work. The Commission notes that the benefits of this provision would extend beyond Social Security, likely reducing Social Security insurance expenditures over the long term.

Conform Eligibility Age for Benefits to Increased Life Span

The Commission recommends indexing the eligibility age for benefits to increased life spans by implementing the following schedule: The already-scheduled increase of two months each year in the normal retirement age, beginning in 2000, would be continued until it reached 70 at the end of 2029. At the same time, the early eligibility age would be increased by two months with each passing year, reaching 65 in 2017. Starting after 2029, each retirement age would be lifted to maintain expected years of retirement at an approximately constant level.

This schedule for increasing the retirement age was included in all four of the Commission's Social Security reform options developed by the Social Security Working Group of the NCRP for consideration by the full Commission. The origin of Social Security's financing problems lie in the demographic shifts that resulted from changes in fertility rates and life expectancy. Consequently, reform proposals that do not address the declining ratio of workers to beneficiaries directly would be likely to see their efficacy diminish over time. The scheduled change in eligibility ages proposed by the NCRP would provide beneficiaries with, relative to other proposed changes that would affect benefits, significant time in which to adjust their retirement planning and also to accrue additional assets through their ISAs.

Current Law

The normal retirement age will rise gradually from 65 to 67, beginning with individuals who reach age 62 in 2000. Early retirement benefits still will be available at age 62 (age 60 for widows and widowers), but at lower levels than under current law.

The proposed increase in the age of eligibility for Social Security benefits is a key element in enabling the Plan to meet the goal of restoring long-term solvency to Social Security.

When Social Security was established in the 1930s the average life expectancy was actually below the age of eligibility (age 65). Since that time, fortunately, the average life span has increased significantly so that average life expectancy today is 76 years. It is expected to rise to 78 by 2020 and continue its upward climb thereafter.

An unchanged age of eligibility for full benefits and an increased life expectancy add greatly to the fiscal pressure on the system over time. Americans are approaching a situation in which they will collect federal health and retirement benefits for an average of one-third of their lives. The Commission proposed to correct this imbalance with a gradual increase in the age of eligibility to keep the average number of years in retirement at approximately the same level over time.

Concern arose that a significant increase in the age of eligibility would present an undue hardship to workers in manual labor jobs. Although this concern is legitimate, it should be kept in mind that major technological and productivity improvements in the economy since the time Social Security was established have greatly reduced blue-collar, physically demanding jobs. Such improvements can be expected to continue in the future. A gradual increase in the age of eligibility to 70 by 2029 would be fair when placed in the perspective that the architects of Social Security deemed 65 an appropriate age of eligibility in the 1930s. For those truly physically unable to continue work, the Commission's Plan would retain a disability program similar to the current program.

The reduced level of benefits for those who opted for the early retirement age called for in the Commission's Plan should be offset by other features of the Plan. Retirement security requires an integrated effort involving Social Security, private pensions, and personal savings equally, so if a worker found it too physically demanding to work beyond the age of eligibility for early retirement benefits, the other two legs of retirement savings (as a reminder, IRA distributions can be made without penalty at age 59½) should more than offset the reduction in benefits produced by the early retirement age benefit differential. Considering the improvements and incentives to save in the Plan, other retirement savings vehicles would have been building assets over time and would be available to help bridge any income gaps necessitated by early retirement.

Critics also cite the difficulty that older workers can have in retaining and finding employment. Although these concerns have a good deal of validity today, a major cause of this situation can be attributed to the relative abundance of younger workers. As the demographics change in the next century, the comparative number of younger replacement workers will decline significantly. The demand for older workers is likely to be strong. Once more, the work incentives incorporated in the Commission's plan, such as adjustment of the early retirement benefit level and delayed retirement credit, would provide further tangible inducements for staying in the workforce longer.

Include State and Local Government Employees in the Social Security System

The Commission recommends covering all state and local government employees hired after 1999.

This provision was included in each of the four plans developed by the Social Security Working Group of the NCRP. Bringing new state and local employees into the Social Security system would contribute to its actuarial stability and is consistent with the philosophical goal of universal national participation in the Social Security program.

Current Law

Currently, approximately one-fourth of state and local government employees are not covered under the OASDI program. In the 1930s, state and local government employees were excluded from the program. In the 1950s, the employees of state and local governments received the opportunity to enter the system. In the 1990s, Congress enacted a law requiring that all public employees not covered by a public retirement plan be covered by Social Security.

Address Inequities between Two-earner and One-earner Couples

The Commission recommends a reduction in the percentage of Primary Insurance Amount (PIA) payable to aged spouse beneficiaries from 50 percent to 33 percent, phased in from 2000 to 2016.

This provision was included in all four plans developed by the Social Security Working Group of the NCRP. The current benefit structure of Social Security provides an inferior rate of return for two-earner couples relative to one-earner couples. The Commission reached the consensus that existing inequities in the program could be addressed by gradually scaling back the benefits in the traditional system that are paid to higher-income one-earner couples and by building additional benefits back into the system for those one-earner couples that most need it through other such measures as the NCRP's minimum benefit provision.

Current Law

Under present law, aged spouses are eligible to receive a benefit equal to 50 percent of their living spouse's PIA, subject to a reduction for their age of retirement.

The Commission supported in principle a revised system of either benefit sharing or earning sharing for married couples that would give each member of the couple equal credit for Social Security taxes during periods in which they were married. The Commission was concerned by the inequity and inefficiency of the current system, which penalizes secondary earners and gives much lower lifetime benefits to couples if their earnings are split fairly evenly (for example, $25,000 each) than if they are unevenly split (for example, $40,000 and $10,000, or $50,000 and 0). In the case of divorce, the current system also gives higher benefits to each of several spouses (and survivors) of a high-income worker than to any sole spouse married to a middle- or low-income worker.

Unfortunately, however, the Commission was not able to find any data on the effects of alternative proposals so that it could determine whether its minimum benefit proposals, which were designed partly to help low-income widows and widowers, were adequate. Nor was the Commission able to determine just how much benefit formulas might have to be adjusted to reach various budget constraints. Therefore, it did not put forward any specific plan but expressed its view that this type of option should be considered as part of any final Social Security reform.

In addition, the Commission believes that a flat (or flatter) benefit payment for retired couples during retirement should be considered so as to provide greater benefits in old age, when poverty and the needs of widows and widowers are likely to rise. This provision interacts with earning sharing options, so, again, the Commission was not able to obtain estimates that would help to determine how to fit the proposal into the base package.

Increase Earnings Years Covered in the AIME Formula to Reflect Longer Working Lives

The Commission recommends that, beginning in 2000, all years of earnings should be counted in the numerator of the Average Indexed Monthly Earnings (AIME) formula, and that the number of computation years in the AIME formula should be increased gradually from 35 to 40 years by adding 1 additional year every 2 years from 2001 to 2010.

The AIME formula should reflect the longer working lives associated with the ultimate increases proposed for the age of eligibility. The Commission also believed, however, that it was important to reward individuals for all the income they had earned, even if it had been on a part-time basis and even if it could not be included among their highest 40 years of lifetime earnings. The Plan proposes that all years of earnings be included in the AIME formula, although the number by which the total was to be divided should remain fixed regardless of how large that number of years turned out to be. The AIME formula no longer would be a true average of highest earnings years but would provide for additional retirement benefits according to every year of covered earnings, no matter how small the income in that particular year.

Current Law

In general, calculating Social Security benefits is a three-step process.

Step One: The Social Security Administration, using Social Security tax records, reconstructs the retiree's wage history. Wages in prior years are indexed by national wage growth to reflect current value. The highest 35 years are selected, averaged, and then divided by 12 to obtain the worker's AIME.

Step Two: Once AIME has been determined, it is plugged into the PIA formula, which is (note that the dollar amounts are indexed and adjusted annually based on the growth in nationwide average annual wages):

❏ add 90 percent of the first $455 of AIME (which equals $5,460 annually);

❏ add 32 percent of AIME between $455 and $2,741; or

❏ add 15 percent of AIME above $2,741.

Step Three: The benefit is adjusted for the age at which the worker is first to receive the benefit (there also are other categories of benefit adjustments and recalculations).

Eliminate the Earnings Test Above the Normal Retirement Age

The Commission recommends eliminating the "earnings test," partly because of the inducement it gives individuals to retire in order to collect some Social Security once they hit an eligible age.

The scoring of the Plan includes only the elimination of the earnings test after the normal retirement age, but retains the effective earnings test between the early and normal retirement age, which, under the agreement, eventually would involve a five-year span. Because the earnings test after the normal retirement age already does not apply after age 70, the long-term impact of this proposal, as currently estimated, would be minimal unless it addressed both types of earnings tests. The Commission was concerned that retaining the harsher of the two existing earnings tests would discourage people from working past the early retirement age.

The Commission believes in principle that the earnings test should be eliminated for all ages but recognized there were some additional scoring issues because its elimination would raise costs in the short run. On the other hand, such a reform actually could reduce long-term deficits if workers responded positively to these and other pro-work aspects of the Plan. The Commission recognized, however, that these changes still could require some modest adjustments in other parts of the proposal so as to strike a reasonable balance between short- and long-term policy goals.

Redirect Social Security Benefit Taxation toward the Social Security Trust Fund

The most recent increase in Social Security benefit taxation was allocated to the Medicare Hospital Insurance (HI) Trust Fund. The Commission recommends gradually returning the income from this benefit taxation back to Social Security, phased in from 2010 to 2019.

This provision was included in all four plans developed by the Social Security Working Group of the NCRP. Although Medicare has more immediate solvency problems than Social Security does, the Commission believed it was undesirable to mix the revenues and outlays for Social Security with those from other programs, even including Medicare, when addressing the solvency of the Social Security system. In order to minimize the adverse impact on Medicare of the return of Social Security benefit taxes to the Social Security system, the Commission recommends gradually phasing in this provision over a period of 10 years.

Adjust Early Retirement Benefits to Reflect Extra Taxes Paid Prior to Retirement

The Commission recommends adjustments to the early retirement benefit level and the delayed retirement credit to reflect more accurately the value of extra taxes paid prior to retirement.

This element was included in each of the four proposals developed by the Social Security Working Group of the NCRP. Current law does not provide a fair deal in all cases for the retiree who waits until the normal retirement age to receive benefits, the actuarial value of which may not exceed early retirement benefits by enough to offset the value of extra taxes paid. The Commission believed Social Security benefits should not bias the decision regarding whether to retire early or late and thus proposes to adjust the ratio of early retirement benefits to normal retirement benefits to reflect the Social Security actuaries' best estimate of the value of additional taxes paid. Consistent with this, the Social Security Working Group would increase the delayed retirement credit, too, to account for the value of additional taxes paid.

Add a "Fail-Safe" Mechanism

The Commission recommends that a "fail-safe" provision be included to prevent unexpected deterioration of Social Security's projected soundness.

This provision also was included in all four plans developed by the Social Security Working Group of the NCRP. Unexpected developments, such as changes in fertility rates or life expectancies, have had—and will continue to have—an effect on projections of Social Security's long-term actuarial solvency. The Commission believed that changes in the program should be required on a timely basis whenever projections showed deteriorating fiscal health in order to prevent delays that could lead to inequitable distribution of the burdens of change. The most appropriate application of this mechanism would be the alteration of the indexing of the eligibility ages after 2029, which could be varied when required in a gradual way in order to maximize both fairness and the time that beneficiaries have to adjust.

Adjust Bend Points

The Commission recommends that bend-point factors of 32 percent and 15 percent would be multiplied by a factor of 0.98 each year from 2001 to 2020.

This provision builds on a similar proposal included in the Social Security Advisory Council's Individual Accounts (IA) Plan. As designed by the Social Security Working Group of the NCRP, this change reflects a belief, first, that the changes in the benefit level to accommodate the carve-out of an individual account should be confined to the top two bend points in order to minimize the impact on low-income retirees; second, that the change should be gradual, phased in by a factor of 2 percent per year, such that each succeeding birth cohort would have received an extra year of accumulation in its ISAs, effecting a gradual transition that would replace unfunded benefits with funded benefits; third, that the changes should enable the traditional Social Security system to survive the retirement of the baby boom generation with a stable Trust Fund.

Current Law

The benefit formula, including the PIA bend points, is explained under the provision to count all years of earnings in the numerator of AIME.

The Commission undertook an extensive analysis of its Plan with the objective of achieving equitable treatment for individuals of different income levels, marital status, and birth cohorts. The Commission outlined the principal objective in such a way that all generations of beneficiaries would share the benefits and the burdens of the system fairly, and the reasonable expectations of those now nearing retirement would be honored.

The 1998 estimates of the Social Security trustees exhibit an improvement in the short-term financial status of the Social Security program relative to 1997 estimates, although the program's long-term fiscal problems remain essentially as before. This improvement creates the opportunity to make further refinements in the Plan that would improve rates of return and replacement rates for retirees early in the twenty-first century, especially those of the baby boom generation. The Commission expected that for subsequent generations of Americans, ISAs would provide a more significant portion of their Social Security income.

The NCRP believed that that the trustees' 1998 reestimates permit further refinements to be made in the Plan on introducing legislation and strengthening the Plan by increasing the retirement income it provides to the baby boom generation. Several members of the Commission favored the option of delaying the effective date of increases in the early eligibility age. Another option was to delay the effective date of the Plan's changes to the 32-percent bend-point factor. (On the congressional front, four Commission members—Judd Gregg [R–N.H.] and John Breaux [D–La.] in the Senate and Jim Kolbe [R–Ariz.] and Charles Stenholm [D–Tex.] in the House of Representatives— introduced the Social Security reform portions of the Commission's Plan [S. 2313 and H.R. 4256, respectively] during the 105th Congress.)

The Commission worked with the Social Security actuaries to produce a preliminary tentative estimate that shows the planned phase-in of changes in the 32-percent bend-point factor could be delayed slightly without harming the stability of the Social Security system. Such a change would increase the replacement rates for near-term retirees in proportion to the number of years of delay. The exact schedule for changes to this bend point and to the early eligibility age should be considered in combination with the other, such that the whole would provide the fairest possible treatment of successive birth cohorts consistent with the overall objective of putting the Social Security system on a sustainable course for all future generations.

The Commission believed that further changes to the Plan could become necessary in order to reduce disparities in replacement rates among birth cohorts to the extent permitted by the 1998 reestimates. The NCRP further noted that some of the elements of the Plan as written actually could increase projected benefits because all the transition periods for benefit changes could not be coordinated fully until the Commission had the opportunity to review actuarial estimates of their combined effect. This led to a small, but unintended, rise in replacement rates for a few cohorts. The NCRP therefore believed that it could become necessary to delay benefit-increasing provisions, such as repealing the earnings limit and counting all years of earnings in the AIME formula, so as to increase the likelihood that transitional benefit changes could be postponed further, and to promote equity among birth cohorts.

Employer-sponsored Private Pension and Personal Savings: Detailed Summary Description

Introduction to Detailed Description

The 21st Century Retirement Security Plan reflects the mission of the NCRP for retirement savings: *National retirement policy should contribute to long-term growth and economic prosperity.* The Retirement Savings portion of the Plan, which includes private pension and personal savings initiatives, complements the Social Security portion to provide a comprehensive program to improve retirement security as a whole.

In the following pages are described the specific proposals included in the Commission's Plan that would enhance the current system of private pensions and personal savings to provide additional retirement income above the floor of support provided by Social Security. These proposals would provide increased opportunities for savings, through both private pension and personal savings arrangements. In addition, they would simplify pension rules to provide understandable options. Portability of benefits would be improved. Most significantly, the proposals would modernize pension provisions to reflect changes in the workforce.

The detailed descriptions that follow not only provide more specificity about the operations of the proposals included in the Commission's Plan, but also compare the proposals to present law and attempt to explain the reasons that the Commission decided to include them in its Plan. In addition, these descriptions are preceded by some background information on private pensions and personal savings to assist in understanding the detailed descriptions, particularly the technical terms of art.

Employer-sponsored Private Pension Savings Summary

Background

Private pension employer-sponsored savings arrangements are accomplished primarily through qualified plans—plans of deferred compensation that meet certain qualification standards of the Internal Revenue Code—that are accorded special tax treatment. Employees do not include qualified plan benefits in gross income until the benefits are distributed, even though the plan is funded and the benefits are nonforfeitable. The employer is entitled to a current deduction (within limits) for contributions to a qualified plan even though the contributions are not included currently in an employee's income. Contributions to a qualified plan are held in a tax-exempt trust.

Employees, as well as employers, may make contributions to a qualified plan. Subject to certain restrictions, employees may make both pre- and after-tax contributions to a qualified plan. Pretax employee contributions—for example, contributions to a qualified cash or deferred arrangement, a 401(k) plan[53]—are treated the same as employer contributions for tax purposes. Qualified plans can be established to provide for salary reduction contributions ("salary reduction plans").

The tax treatment of contributions under qualified plans is essentially the same as that of deductible IRAs. The limits on contributions to qualified plans are much higher, however, than the IRA contribution limits so that qualified plans provide for a greater accumulation of funds on a tax-favored basis. The policy rationale for permitting greater accumulation under qualified plans than under IRAs is that the tax benefits for qualified plans encourage employers to provide benefits for a broad group of their employees. This reduces the need for public assistance and reduces pressure on the Social Security system.

The current qualification standards and related rules governing qualified plans are designed to ensure that qualified plans benefit an employer's rank-and-file employees as well as its highly compensated employees. They also define the rights of plan participants and beneficiaries and provide limits on the tax benefits for qualified plans. A certain number of rules relating to qualified plans are designed to ensure that the amounts contributed to qualified plans are used for retirement purposes. Thus, for example, an early withdrawal tax applies to premature distributions from such plans and the ability to obtain distributions prior to the termination of employment from certain types of qualified plans is restricted.

Types of Qualified Plans

Qualified plans are classified into two broad categories, defined-benefit plans and defined-contribution plans, based on the nature of the benefits provided.

Under a defined-benefit pension plan, benefit levels are specified under a plan formula. For example, a defined-benefit pension plan might provide an annual retirement benefit of 2 percent of final average compensation multiplied by total years of service completed by an employee. Benefits under a defined-benefit pension plan are funded by the general assets of the trust established under the plan; individual accounts are not maintained for employees participating in the plan. Benefits under a defined-benefit pension plan are guaranteed (within limits) by the Pension Benefit Guaranty Corporation (PBGC), a federal corporation within the Department of Labor.

Benefits under defined-contribution plans are based solely on the contributions (and earnings thereon) allocated to separate accounts maintained for each plan participant. Profit-sharing plans and qualified cash or deferred arrangements—

---

53. Many qualified plans are described by the section of the Internal Revenue Code that establishes the plan—for example, 401(k), 403(b), and 457—and are described similarly herein.

401(k) plans—are examples of defined-contribution plans.

The Commission's Plan makes a number of changes to private pension employer-sponsored savings arrangements. These changes include:

- ❑ a universal 401(k) plan;
- ❑ improved defined-benefit plans;
- ❑ enhanced pension portability;
- ❑ increased savings opportunities;
- ❑ the modernization of pension provisions to reflect changes in the workforce;
- ❑ additional improvements; and
- ❑ other proposals.

Create a Universal 401(k) Plan

Current Law. Under current law, complex rules base eligibility for salary reduction–qualified plans on the type of employer. These different salary-reduction plans include 401(k) plans, which generally can be adopted by corporations and other for-profit organizations; 403(b) plans, which can be adopted by certain not-for-profit organizations; and 457 plans, which can be adopted by state and local governments.

Commission's Recommendation. Establish a single type of salary reduction–qualified retirement plan—a "universal 401(k) plan"—available to all employers, regardless of type. All types of employers could (but would not be required to) convert their existing 403(b) and 457 plans into 401(k) plans. The law would not be changed for 403(b) and 457 plans.

Rationale. Different types of salary reduction–qualified plans were developed at different times for different types of employers. Over time, the differences among these types of plans have diminished, but important differences remain. The Commission believed no good public policy explanations exist as to the reasons these differences should continue. The Commission's review of Internal Revenue Service (IRS) data and opinion surveys led it to the conclusion that confusion about different types of plans prevents employers from establishing retirement plans and employees from participating in plans or continuing to maintain their retirement savings in plans on job changes.

Improve Defined-Benefit Plans

Current Law. Under current law, complex funding and accrual rules apply to defined-benefit plans. In addition, pension portability has been difficult to achieve with defined-benefit plans because of their inability to transfer accrued benefits from one job to another without converting such benefits to a lump sum.

Small employers that wish to establish a tax-favored retirement savings plan without significant costs and complexity may establish a "simple" plan under current law. A simple plan is a defined-contribution plan that can come in the form of a Simple IRA or Simple 401(k) plan. These simple plans are not subject to many of the rules applicable to qualified plans, but are subject only to minimal reporting and disclosure requirements. Currently no alternative to Simple plans is available for the small employer that seeks to provide its workers with a simplified, tax-favored, defined-benefit plan.

Commission's Recommendation. Establish a defined-benefit equivalent to the simple plan so that the small employer that prefers a defined-benefit alternative could create one on a cost-effective basis. The Simple Defined-Benefits Plan would have the following characteristics:

❐ **Employer eligibility**—Small businesses with 100 or fewer employees would be eligible, including professional service employers (for example, doctors, lawyers, and engineers). Employers, however, must not have had a defined-benefit or defined-contribution plan for the previous five years.

❐ **Individual eligibility**—All employees would be eligible if they had two years of prior service and were earning at least $5,000 in compensation in the current year.

❐ **Vesting**—All contributions would be 100-percent vested.

❐ **Nondiscrimination rules and reporting requirements**—Most nondiscrimination limitations and requirements would be waived.

❐ **Minimum defined benefit and size of account**—Each participant would have a separate account, as in a defined-contribution plan. The minimum defined benefit would have to equal 1 or 2 percent of compensation for that year. An employer could elect to increase that benefit to 3 percent of compensation for the first five years of the plan. All employees would have to receive the same level of benefits.

❐ **Past service credit**—There would be a five-year past service credit that would have to be funded over an equal number of years.

❐ **Considered compensation**—Current law would be followed; it states that the annual compensation limit that can be taken into account for qualified retirement plan purposes is $160,000 indexed.

❐ **PBGC**—There would be no required PBGC benefit.

❐ **Termination**—Because each participant's benefit would be kept in a separate account, benefits would be fully portable because distribution of the separate account in a lump sum could not affect remaining participants adversely. On termination of employment, benefits could be transferred to an annuity or regular IRA; otherwise, they would become subject to an early distribution penalty tax of 20 percent.

Rationale. From its review of IRS data and opinion surveys, the Commission concluded that defined benefit plans are underutilized because of overly complex funding rules and portability obstacles. The number of defined-benefit plans in small and medium-sized employers has decreased substantially. The Commission believed a Simple Defined-Benefit Plan, in particular, would overcome these problems with its hybrid approach that would provide a level of guaranteed investment return while giving participants the benefit of possible additional return. Increased use of defined-benefit plans also could help the large numbers of baby boomers who have inadequate retirement savings and are running out of years to save.

Enhance Pension Portability

Current Law. Under current law, pension portability is not permitted between different types of plans (between 401(k) and 403(b) plans, for example). In addition, IRC–411(d)(6) prohibits transferee plans from accepting transfers from other plans without offering benefits, such as distribution options, peculiar to the transferor plan.

Commission's Recommendation. Take action on the following recommendations from the Retirement Account Portability (RAP) Act of 1998 (H.R. 3503), introduced by Representatives Earl Pomeroy (D–N.D.) and Kolbe.

❑ **Section 457 plans.** State and local government employees typically have access to a tax-deferred compensation plan called a 457 plan. Section 2 of RAP for the first time would allow these employees to roll over funds from their 457 plans into IRAs or into the retirement plans of their new employers when they switched jobs. Section 2 of RAP also would allow workers moving from the for-profit and nonprofit sectors into state and local government to roll over their retirement savings from their prior jobs into the section 457 plan available at their new state or local government workplace.

❑ **Section 403(b) plans.** Section 403(b) plans are tax-deferred retirement plans available to the employees of many nonprofit entities and public school systems. Section 2 of RAP for the first time would allow these employees to roll over funds from their 403(b) plans into the retirement plan of their new for-profit or state/local government employer when they switched jobs. Section 2 also would allow workers moving from a for-profit or state/local government job to a job that offers a 403(b) plan to roll over their retirement savings from their prior job into the 403(b) plan.

❑ **No employer mandates.** Even though RAP would remove the legal obstacles that have prevented rollovers in the situations described above, it contains no mandates that require employers to accept rollovers from their new employees. Thus, under RAP, a rollover would occur whenever the employee chose to move the money and whenever the employer agreed to accept it.

☐ **Expanded-conduit IRAs.** Under current law, employees who switch jobs but cannot or do not roll over their retirement savings into a plan at a new workplace may place the money into a special IRA called a "conduit IRA." So long as they do not add other contributions to this conduit IRA, the funds inside it can be rolled back into a workplace retirement plan at a later date. Under current law, however, a conduit IRA is severely limited with respect to the types of workplace retirement plan money it can accept and the types of workplace retirement plans into which its funds can be transferred later. Section 3 of RAP would correct this problem by allowing workers to move any kind of defined-contribution plan money into a conduit IRA and then allowing this money to be rolled back into any variety of defined-contribution plan.

☐ **Consolidation of deductible IRA contributions.** Section 3 also would allow many individuals to consolidate their IRA funds and their workplace retirement savings in a single place. Under Section 3 of RAP, individuals who had IRAs and whose IRA contributions all had been tax deductible would have the opportunity to transfer funds from their IRAs into their workplace retirement plan—provided that the retirement plan trustee met the same high standards as an IRA trustee.

☐ **Rollovers of after-tax contributions.** Although pretax contributions to retirement plans are perhaps the most common form of employee contribution, many plans also allow participants to make after-tax contributions. Under current law, these after-tax contributions cannot be rolled over when employees switch jobs, meaning that workers face the confusing prospect of being able to roll over their pretax money but not their after-tax money. Section 4 of RAP would allow individuals for the first time to roll over their after-tax contributions to their new employer's plan or to an IRA so long as the plan or IRA provider agreed to track and report the after-tax portion of the rollover for the individual.

☐ **Rationalization of the restrictions on distributions from defined-contribution plans.** Under current law, when a business is sold but an employee continues to work in the same role for the new employer, he can transfer much of his retirement money to the retirement plans of the new company. Under the "same-desk rule," however, this transfer is not permitted for funds in such defined-contribution plans as 401(k)s, requiring the employee to leave the money in his former employer's plan. Section 8 of RAP could repeal the same-desk rule so that the entire amount of a worker's retirement funds could be transferred to the new employer's plan after the corporate sale took place.

❏ **Transferee defined-contribution plans would not need to have the same distribution options as transferor defined-contribution plans.** One barrier to portability under current law is that employees are restricted from transferring funds from a defined-contribution plan in which they used to participate to their new employer's defined-contribution plan if the new plan does not have the same benefit options as the old plan. Under section 9 of RAP, employees and their spouses who wished to transfer their funds to the new employer's plan could choose to do so even in cases in which the benefit options differed.

❏ **Allowance for employers to disregard rollovers for purposes of cashout amounts.** Under current law, employers are allowed to cash out the retirement benefits of departing employees when these benefits are valued at less than $5,000. This reduces the administrative burden that otherwise would be placed on employers by management of many small retirement plan accounts. Section 10 of RAP would make clear that, in determining whether employees' benefit levels fall below the $5,000 cashout threshold, employers would not need to take into account any benefits that the employee had rolled over from a prior job. Thus, employers would need only to evaluate the ways in which retirement benefits earned at their own workplace compared with the $5,000 threshold. Without Section 10, employers might be reluctant to accept rollovers because they could be forced to maintain accounts even for workers who exceeded the $5,000 threshold only by virtue of the money they had brought with them from a prior job.

❏ **Purchase of service credits in governmental defined-benefit plans.** Employees of state and local governments, particularly teachers, often move between states and school districts in the course of their careers. Under state law, these employees often have the option of purchasing service credits in their state defined-benefit pension plans in order to make up for time spent in another state or district. With purchase of these service credits, workers can earn a pension reflecting a full career of employment in the state in which they conclude their career. Under current law, these employees are not able to use the money they have saved in their 403(b) or 457 defined-contribution plans to purchase these service credits and often lack other resources to use for this purpose. Under Section 10 of RAP, state and local government employees for the first time would be able to use funds from these retirement savings plans to purchase service credits and earn a full defined-benefit pension.

Rationale. Leakage of money out of retirement savings vehicles continues to present a barrier to adequate retirement income savings. This problem is particularly acute in cases in which individuals change jobs and are not permitted to carry over or consolidate their private pension employer-sponsored arrangements. Although prior tax law changes significantly reduced leakage, barriers to pension portability still exist. All the changes described above will help to keep funds in the private pension system.

Increase Opportunities to Save

Give a Tax Credit to Small Employers. Current Law. An employer's costs related to the establishment of a retirement plan (for example, payroll system changes, investment vehicle setup fees, consulting fees, and so forth) generally are deductible (and not creditable) as ordinary business expenses.

    Commission's Recommendation. Commission's Plan would provide a tax credit to small employers that adopt an employer-sponsored retirement plan for the first time. As is the case in the Clinton administration's legislative proposals for the fiscal year 1999 budget, the tax credit would be limited to 50 percent of up to $2,000 of administrative and retirement-education expenses in the first year of the plan and to 50 percent of up to $1,000 of such expenses in each of the second and third years.[54]

    Rationale. The costs associated with plan startup, plan administration, and retirement education could pose a barrier to the establishment of new retirement programs, especially for smaller employers. Providing a tax credit for creating new plans could promote their adoption, not only by defraying some of these costs but also by providing a marketing tool for financial institutions or advisers to use in promoting new program adoption and by increasing awareness of retirement savings options.

Create a Catch-up Provision. Current Law. Under current law, taxpayers who are unemployed or choose to be out of the workforce to raise a family generally cannot contribute to retirement savings accounts in a qualified plan. Moreover, when these individuals rejoin the workforce, there is no ability to make up for missed retirement savings contributions.

    Commission's Recommendation. Commission's Plan would allow individuals who had not been a participant under a qualified plan for the past five calendar years and with an income of less than $50,000 in the current year to contribute an additional $2,000 ($4,000 total) into their IRA or ISA for up to five years (that is, a total of $10,000 in additional contributions). These additional voluntary contributions would not be eligible for a tax credit or a matching contribution, respectively.

    Rationale. The Plan would target the additional contribution limits more accurately at those who were most in need of the additional flexibility while providing an additional vehicle for such savings (for example, the ISA).

Repeal the 25-percent Compensation under Internal Revenue Code 415(c)(1)(B). Current Law. Under current law, total employee contributions to a tax-qualified defined-contribution plan are limited to the lesser of 25 percent of compensation or $30,000.

---

54. See U.S. Department of the Treasury, *General Explanations of the Administration's Revenue Proposals,* February 1998.

Commission's Recommendation. The Commission's Plan would repeal the 25-percent limit

Rationale. The 25-percent-of-compensation limit hinders middle-income Americans from making contributions up to the dollar limit in years in which they otherwise have the ability to do so. The 415(c) limit as currently structured provides a higher threshold of savings for higher-paid workers—the operative limit for higher-paid workers is $30,000. Eliminating the 25-percent limit would allow lower-paid workers to be subject similarly to the $30,000 limit only. This would help lower-paid women and others to save in a tax-preferred manner. Lifting the 25-percent limit would not be a windfall for highly paid workers because the Internal Revenue Code contains other limitations that provide against abuse, such as nondiscrimination testing.

Modernize Pension Provisions to Reflect the Changing Nature of the Workforce

Faster Vesting. Current Law. Under current law, employer matching contributions made by employers to defined-contribution plans must be either 100-percent vested after five years or gradually vested in increments over seven years.

Commission's Recommendation. The Commission's Plan would reduce the minimum vesting requirements to provide that 100 percent of benefits be vested within three years or gradually vested in increments over six years.

Rationale. Considering the mobile nature of today's workforce, there is the significant risk that many participants will leave employment before fully vesting in an employer's matching contributions to a defined-contribution plan. One way to increase the portability of benefits for participants in defined-contribution plans—for example, 401(k) plans—is to require faster vesting for employer matching contributions.

Flexibility for Partial Retirement. Current Law. In general, individuals may access their pension benefits only through full retirement, death, disability, or separation of service.

Commission's Recommendation. The Commission's Plan would provide additional flexibility for individuals to access a portion of their accrued pension benefits when they are eligible for retirement but continue to work part-time for the same employer (for example, based on the early retirement age under the plan but no earlier than 59½).

Rationale. An increasing number of workers is easing out of the workforce through part-time employment instead of going from full-time employment to full-time retirement. Giving individuals the opportunity to access a portion of their pension benefits would encourage continued part-time employment. This change would apply only to those working part-time for the same employer because a broader application could encourage individuals to retire early.

Additional Improvements for All Plans. Current Law. The government's rules that apply to all plans, not just 401(k) plans, have become increasingly complex. In some cases, this complexity is misplaced. For example, employers are required to make unnecessary filings with the government but are not required to provide periodic statements of benefits to participants. Plan participants are allowed to request only certain information regarding their accrued benefits once each year.

Commission's Recommendation. The Commission's Plan would simplify and rationalize existing rules applicable to all plans by

❑ requiring defined-benefit and defined-contribution plans to provide periodic benefit statements to plan participants; and

❑ allowing employers to take advantage of new technologies, such as the Internet, to meet various notice, consent, and similar requirements.

The Plan would require that participants in defined-benefit pension and defined-contribution savings plans periodically receive certain information concerning their individual accrued benefits under their benefits plan. Specifically, it would require that participants in defined-contribution plans be provided with a summary of their account balance and vesting status at least annually, and that participants in defined-benefit plans be provided with a summary of their accrued benefits and vested status every three years. Plan sponsors would receive the flexibility to provide the above information to inactive plan participants on request if they provided a summary of the same information at the time the participant separates from service. Plan sponsors also would receive the flexibility to meet this requirement either through electronic or nonelectronic forms of communication.

Rationale. The Commission believed that, as a general rule, complexity hinders pension plan coverage and retirement income adequacy. As a result, the Commission concluded that reporting and disclosure rules should be focused more acutely on educating plan participants and using the latest available technology to do so in order to increase pension coverage and enable participants to achieve increased retirement income adequacy.

Most defined-contribution plans—especially those with participant-directed investments—provide information regarding the participant's accrued benefits at least annually, either in writing or through electronic access. Defined-contribution plans are not required to provide this service, however, and not all plans do. Accrued benefit information is the most important information a participant can receive. Receiving this information can help to assure the accuracy and integrity of the plan's records and facilitate retirement planning by plan participants.

Many defined-benefit plans, especially multiemployer plans, never provide accrued benefit information to a plan participant until he applies for a benefit. Participants in these plans should be provided with selected accrued benefit information at least every three years in order to help assure the integrity of the plan's records and to assist them in their efforts to plan their retirement.

Other Proposals

Revise Current IRS Tax Qualification Sanctions. Current Law. The IRS has the ability to disqualify a plan for violations of the operational requirements applicable to qualified retirement and savings plans. The IRS also has broad discretion as to the point at which to disqualify a plan and the related trust.

Although actual disqualification is rare, the IRS typically uses the economic sanctions that could occur on disqualification as a factor in determining the appropriate penalty.

Commission's Recommendation. The Commission's Plan would revise the sanctions available to the IRS for violations of the operational requirements applicable to qualified retirement and savings plans as follows:

❐ No economic sanction would be imposed if the violation had been fully corrected prior to any related IRS audit;

❐ The IRS would receive the ability to impose a sanction of up to 20 percent of the actual damage amount for violations that it had discovered and that the sponsor had corrected within agreed-on time frames. The IRS would be able to impose a sanction of up to 100 percent of the actual damage amount if the sponsor had failed to correct the violations within the agreed-on time frame; and

❐ The IRS would be allowed to disqualify a plan or trust in cases in which the sponsor had engaged in known, material, and recurring violations of the tax qualification requirements.

Rationale. Although the IRS has promulgated a number of voluntary compliance programs over the past several years, a revision of the sanctions associated with tax qualifications issues is appropriate to provide reasonable deterrents to abuse and additional consistency in enforcement actions while avoiding excessive fines or discretion on behalf of the IRS. The proposed sanction approach is generally consistent with the sanctions provided to the Department of Labor in connection with fiduciary breaches and the IRS in connection with prohibited transactions.

Strengthen the Antialienation Provisions Associated with Qualified Retirement and Savings Plans.
Current Law. Participant benefits under qualified pension and savings plans are provided certain protections against antialienation.

Commission's Recommendation. The Commission's Plan would provide for total protection of accrued benefits under qualified plans except in cases of fiduciary breaches by a fiduciary who has accrued benefits under the plan that was the subject of the breach. This provision would not serve to prevent the proper splitting of pension assets in connection with a divorce.

Rationale. Providing strong protection for pension assets would serve to encourage savings through qualified plans within applicable limits.

Preservation of Retirement Assets for Retirement.
Current Law. Current law does not encourage or require employer and employee contributions to be preserved for retirement purposes only.

Commission's Recommendation. The Commission's Plan would change current law to require that certain employer contributions and a certain percentage of employee contributions be preserved for retirement, death, or permanent disability. The specific proposals would require that

❐ *non-deminimis* distributions related to employer contributions be rolled over and preserved until retirement (possibly at age 59½), death, or permanent disability; and

❐ a stated percentage (for example, 50 percent) of employee deferrals be preserved until retirement, death, or permanent disability. As to the remaining percentage (for example, the other 50 percent), the proposal would drop the excise tax on early distributions and allow loans without triggering any tax consequences.

Rationale. Current law does not ensure that retirement savings are used for retirement purposes. Requiring that certain employer contributions and a certain percentage of employee contributions be preserved for retirement, death, or permanent disability would guarantee that at least a portion of both employer and employee contributions to retirement plans are available at the time when needed.

Personal Savings Summary: Broad Simplification of IRAs

Simplify IRAs

Current Law. Americans who meet certain Adjusted Gross Income (AGI) qualifications can save personally through contributions to deductible IRAs and Roth IRAs. These AGI limitations are not uniform, and this lack of uniformity causes great complexity and confusion. Americans who do not meet these limits can save through contributions to nondeductible IRAs.

❐ **Deductible IRAs:** Currently, an individual may make deductible contributions to an IRA up to the lesser of $2,000 or his compensation if he is not an active participant in an employer-sponsored retirement plan. In the case of a married couple, deductible IRA contributions of up to $2,000 can be made for each spouse (including, for example, a homemaker who does not work outside the home) if the combined compensation of both spouses is at least equal to the contributed amount.

If the individual (or his spouse) is an active participant in an employer-sponsored retirement plan, the $2,000 deduction limit is phased out for tax-payers with AGI over certain levels for the taxable year.

The phaseout limits for a single individual who is an active participant in an employer-sponsored retirement plan are as follows: for 1998, $30,000 to $40,000; for 1999, 2000, 2001, and 2002, the limits increase by $1,000 each year until they are, by 2002, $34,000 to $44,000; for 2003, $40,000 to $50,000; for 2004, $45,000 to $55,000; and for 2005 and thereafter, $50,000 to $60,000.

The phaseout limits for a married individual filing a joint return who is an active participant in an employer-sponsored plan are as follows: for 1998, $50,000 to $60,000; for 1999, 2000, 2001, and 2002, the limits

increase by $1,000 each year, so that the limits by 2002 are $54,000 to
$64,000, for 2003, $60,000 to $70,000; for 2004, $65,000 to $75,000; for
2005, $70,000 to $80,000; for 2006, $75,000 to $85,000; and for 2007 and
thereafter, $80,000 to $90,000.

In the case of a married taxpayer filing a separate return, the deduction
is phased out between $0 and $10,000 of AGI. The maximum deductible
IRA contribution for an individual who is not an active participant but
whose spouse *is* an active participant is phased out for taxpayers with AGI
between $150,000 and $160,000.

❑ **Roth IRAs:** For years beginning in 1998, individuals with AGI below
certain levels may make nondeductible contributions to a Roth IRA. The
maximum annual contribution that can be made to a Roth IRA is the lesser
of $2,000 or the individual's compensation for the year. The contribution
limit is reduced to the extent that an individual makes contributions to any
other IRA in the same taxable year. As under the rules relating to IRAs
generally, a contribution of up to $2,000 for each spouse may be made to a
Roth IRA, provided that the combined compensation of the spouses is at
least equal to the contributed amount. The maximum annual contribution
that can be made to a Roth IRA is phased out for single individuals with
AGI between $95,000 and $110,000 and for joint filers with AGI between
$150,000 and $160,000.

❑ **Nondeductible IRAs:** To the extent that an individual cannot or does not
make deductible contributions to an IRA or contributions to a Roth IRA, the
individual can make nondeductible contributions to an IRA.

Commission's Recommendation. The Commission's Plan sets a universal
AGI limit for all IRAs (except the nondeductible IRA). The Plan does not specify
the dollar amount at which income limits should be set until a cost estimate is done
because revenue effects for various alternatives were not obtainable. The
Commission anticipates, however, that universal limits would be achieved by
phasing up the traditional IRA income limits to mirror the Roth IRA income limits.
In addition, the $2,000 contribution limit would be indexed.

Rationale. From its review of IRS data and opinion surveys, the Commission saw
that complexity and resulting confusion among Americans will keep IRA
utilization low, despite the clear desire of Congress and the Clinton administration
to expand their usage. Since restrictions were placed on IRA eligibility in 1986, the
level of IRA usage has dropped from 17 percent to 7 percent. Although the Roth
IRA increased IRA usage in 1998, confusion about eligibility remains a barrier to
IRA utilization, and IRA usage has dropped at all income levels. Although the
Commission endorsed simplification of IRAs, it did not believe IRAs are intended
to replace the current employer-sponsored retirement plans. The multiple "pillars"
(private savings, Social Security, and employer-sponsored plans) that provide for
retirement security should be retained and strengthened.

Social Security: Assumptions

The Plan assumes the implementation of reforms to the consumer price index (CPI) that will reduce it by 0.5 percent below projections in the *1997 Annual Report of the Board of Trustees of the Federal Old-Age and Survivors Insurance and Disability Insurance Trust Funds.* The Bureau of Labor Statistics (BLS) has made several improvements in the calculation of the CPI to address previous overstatement, and continues to make adjustments. The BLS already has announced changes that will result in a reduction of 0.17 percent in the CPI lower-level substitution bias by implementing a geometric mean aggregation procedure in most categories. The Commission believed the BLS can make additional improvements in the accuracy of the CPI, particularly in the area of upper-level substitution bias, that would result in a reduction of at least an additional 0.33 percent in the CPI necessary to meet the 0.5 percent assumption. The Commission supported the efforts of Congress and the Clinton administration to encourage the BLS to continue to improve the CPI and to provide the BLS with the necessary resources and authority to do so.

For purposes of scoring the increases in the normal retirement age and the early eligibility age, each is presumed to increase by two months every three years after 2029.

The Commission was careful to provide for minimal changes for those expecting to retire soon while, at the same time, beginning to build up some savings for those who were younger. The proposal, as modeled by the actuaries, would establish individual savings accounts only for individuals younger than 55 when the provisions became effective. Consequently, the danger would arise of differential treatment of a worker aged 54 years and 11 months relative to a worker aged 55. Lacking the resources to rescore several different methods of avoiding the creation of a benefit "notch," the Commission acknowledged that an adjustment could be required here, but it also noted that any adjustment in the availability of a private account would require simultaneously some adjustment in the speed at which benefit changes were made to provide for the fairest possible treatment of subsequent birth cohorts.

The Impact on the Unified Federal Budget

The Commission believed its Plan would have a significant positive impact by reducing the long-term debt of the federal government by addressing the unfunded long-term liabilities of the Social Security Trust Fund. The Commission became certain that the long-term benefits clearly justified the modest short-term deficits in the unified budget to fund the transition costs of a reform plan. Improved budget projections suggest, however, that this Plan could be enacted without requiring an increase in federal borrowing from the public.

The Commission considered it essential for Congress to preserve the opportunity to enact Social Security reform with minimal impact on the short-term borrowing from the public by restraining itself from "spending the surplus" in other ways until it had the chance to evaluate the extent to which a unified budget could help to offset the transition costs of its Plan. A critical opportunity to reform and strengthen Social Security, and to reduce the long-term debt obligations of the federal government, would be lost if Congress acted hastily to reduce or eliminate projected unified federal budget surpluses before acting on Social Security reform.

Social Security: Administering and Regulating Individual Security Accounts

The 21st Century Retirement Security Plan assumes a design of individual security accounts that is analogous to the Thrift Savings Plan (TSP) provided to federal retirees.

Administrative concerns argue strongly for working within the current payroll tax collection structure to direct contributions on behalf of covered workers into ISAs. Currently, employers typically pay payroll taxes on behalf of each employee on a biweekly basis and report total contributions to the Social Security Administration at the end of each year. To minimize costs, the Commission's Plan assumes that the responsibilities of employers should remain roughly the same as under current law. The NCRP recommends that the burden of record-keeping for each individual be assumed by a bureau within the Social Security Administration created for and dedicated to this purpose, with the administrative costs distributed proportionally among ISAs. This Plan assumes administrative costs of 10 basis points for such a system, based on estimates provided by the Social Security actuaries. The Commission recognized that some financing would be needed and amortized over a 20-year period because there would be startup costs and the ISA would not reach a size to achieve the economies of scale contemplated for a number of years. The Plan would provide for legislative enactment in 1999 and implementation of the ISAs one year after the date of enactment. The Commission also recognized, however, that the establishment of ISAs would present significant administrative challenges, and that the timeframe for implementing ISAs must be conditioned on administrative feasibility.

Minimizing employer burdens are but one reason for adopting a TSP-style structure. Because of the small balances that would exist within the accounts of low-income employees, it is essential that administrative costs not be of a size to destroy an individual's capacity to receive a positive net rate of return from his investment. A decentralized mechanism in which low-income individuals were obliged to set up their accounts privately and individually as with IRA accounts would be likely to result in higher administrative costs.

Investment choices for these ISAs would be provided in a manner similar to the existing TSP. Investors could choose among such broad-based funds as, for example, stock index funds based on the Wilshire 5000 or the Standard & Poor's 500; a bond index fund; a blended index fund that includes both stocks and bonds; and a government securities fund. Wage-earners under 45 years of age who failed to specify an investment fund at the startup of the ISA regime would be provided a standard blend of 50 percent U.S. Treasury bonds and 50 percent Standard & Poor's 500 Index equities. Those 45 years and older at the startup of the ISA regime would be placed into the treasury bond option. The bond option for those entering over age 45 would be phased out over a 20-year period. After about 2020, the blended option would become the only standard option.

The Commission envisions that after a few years an increased number of investment options would be provided to beneficiaries. For each type of portfolio, investors would have the choice between various government-approved companies to manage the funds within the TSP model. Firms would bid competitively for the right to manage these funds, with an eye toward minimizing administrative costs.

Once the system became operational, the Commission recommends that additional voluntary contributions be permitted to ISAs and that Congress consider providing incentives to enable individuals of all income levels to benefit from this option. Congress also should consider, once the system had matured to the point at which administrative costs became predictable and manageable, allowing rollover contributions from these personal accounts into ISAs so long as they featured the same withdrawal rules as the ISAs, provided that these accounts were invested in broadly diversified accounts with low administrative costs.

Individual funds would be fully vested, and an individual would have a non-forfeitable property right in contributions to his account and in earnings accrued. No access would be allowed to the account until retirement, and even then only within the guidelines prescribed by the program's rollover and distribution rules. Record-keeping for ISAs must be explicit and make clear to individuals that earnings posted to their accounts are direct market earnings, net of administrative expense, from direct investment of pooled account assets in financial instruments.

The fund managers would have the fiduciary responsibility for standards of management and investment of assets. The fiduciary provisions should recognize an "exclusive benefit" rule, which would assure each wage-earner that account contributions could be used only for the purpose of providing retirement savings for that individual: the government would have no ability to utilize account contributions or earnings. In addition, the Commission recommends the creation of a comprehensive regulatory program for the oversight of asset managers, allowing for a reasonable self-regulation by the investment industry.

Social Security is intended as a safety net that provides a retiree with a monthly income for as long as he lives. ISAs should not change the basic nature of the system. Combined with traditional Social Security, these accounts should provide a retiree with income security for the rest of his life.

The Commission opposed withdrawal rules, such as preretirement or lump-sum distributions, that would expose individual beneficiaries to increased risk of poverty, relative to protections that would have existed had ISAs not been established. Therefore, the Plan prohibits preretirement withdrawals other than for death or disability.

On retirement, individuals would be required to annuitize that portion of their ISA balances that, when added to their traditional Social Security benefit, were necessary to provide an income comfortably above the poverty level. Individuals would be able to choose between a number of annuity plans that reflected the life needs of the individual. Individuals would not be required to withdraw non-annuitized balances on retirement.

The annuities would be similar to those required to be offered to plan participants under qualified defined-benefit plans subject to the Employee Retirement Income Security Act (ERISA) and would be indexed for inflation. Under ERISA, if the retiree is married, the normal benefit form is a joint and survivor annuity. In order to assure that the monthly payments kept pace with increases in the cost of living, the annuities could be adjusted for inflation annually, perhaps through the use of the treasury indexed bonds. Individuals would be able to choose from a group of insurance companies that had been selected in a competitive bidding process for the right to manage these accounts. A government-provided standard option would be available as well.

Concerns about shorter life expectancies among the poor could be addressed by requiring either a life annuity, period certain (income for life is promised but a minimum number of payments is guaranteed) or a refund annuity (monthly payments continue after death until the combined benefits have equaled the purchase price of the annuity).

Social Security: Three Additional Reform Plans

The Social Security Working Group of the NCRP developed four plans that would meet the criteria for Social Security reform established by the Commission. The other three include the following.

"Defined Benefit Plan"

This plan would balance the traditional Social Security program and preserve its defined-benefit character but would not include a personal defined-contribution account. It also would:

❑ raise the normal retirement age to 70 by 2029, the early retirement age to 65 by 2017, and index both after 2029 in order to maintain expected years of retirement at an approximately constant level;

❑ cover all state and local government employees hired after 1999;

❑ reduce the percentage of PIA payable to aged spouse beneficiaries from 50 percent to 33 percent (phased in from 2000 to 2016);

❑ beginning in 2000, count all years of earnings in the numerator of AIME;

❑ eliminate the earnings test;

❑ credit all revenue from the taxation of benefits to OASDI (phase revenue from HI to OASDI between 2010 and 2019);

❑ include lost tax revenues in actuarial adjustment for early/late retirement;

❑ create a "fail-safe" mechanism to protect the program against variations from assumptions; and

❑ institute a minimum benefit provision to begin in full in 2010, with initial benefit protection wage-indexed thereafter.

"Defined Benefit–Plus" Plan

Provisions are the same as in the defined-benefit plan, except that an "add-on" personal account would be established with contributions above the 12.4 percent payroll tax rate. For purposes of illustration, the account is assumed to be a mandated savings account of size equal to 2 percent of taxable payroll.

"ISA-Plus" Plan

Provisions to balance the traditional Social Security system are identical to the 21st Century Retirement Security Plan, except that the payroll tax refund into personal accounts would apply only to individuals under age 55, and an additional contribution of 2 percent would be required so that the personal accounts be funded at a level of 4 percent of taxable payroll.

Social Security: Why This Plan Among the Four Alternatives?

Each of the four plans developed by the Social Security Working Group of the NCRP achieves the goals developed by the Commission for reform of the Social Security program.

The Commission considered the approach taken in the 21st Century Retirement Security Plan as the best choice on the grounds both of policy and of political feasibility. The arguments for selecting the plan over the defined-benefit proposal could be summarized as follows:

1. The Plan, due to the inclusion of a personal account, would improve rates of return and therefore increase retirement income for most beneficiaries, relative to a package of purely traditional solutions.

2. The Plan would fund in advance a portion of the future liabilities of the Social Security system and thus place a smaller tax burden on the future economy than the defined-benefit plan, increasing the flexibility for future Americans to address other national needs or crises.

3. The Plan simultaneously would improve returns for beneficiaries and reduce long-term federal liabilities in principal and interest to the Social Security Trust Fund, relative to a purely defined-benefit solution.

Finally, the leading argument in favor of a defined-benefit solution over a personal account solution has been much diminished in force in recent times due to improved projections for the federal unified budget balance. Current budget predictions indicate that the federal government could create accounts equal to 2 percent of national taxable payroll without incurring a unified budget deficit. This would create the opportunity that the chairs believe should be seized to limit future federal liabilities that could not be accomplished if the federal government continued to invest surplus OASDI revenues in treasury securities.

The chairs noted that it is possible to produce a rate of return for beneficiaries that is higher than the Plan would provide, providing that additional contributions be required as in the "Defined Benefit–Plus" or "ISA-Plus" plans. It was the judgment of the chairs, however, that requiring such an additional contribution would be tantamount to a tax increase, and that allowing additional voluntary contributions, therefore, would provide the best way to maximize individual rates of return. The chairs urged that all proposals be viewed not in isolation, but in the context of other pressing national needs, including the necessity of devoting additional funding to Medicare and to private retirement systems. Consequently, the Commission believed the Plan, as drafted, represents the best choice because it achieves the Commission's stated objectives without an effective increase in taxation.

Social Security: An Explanation of Distributional Effects

One additional reason for supporting the 21st Century Retirement Security Plan over the alternatives is the greater degree of progressivity that it would achieve. The most significant reason for this effect is the progressive method of changing the PIA formula to carve out the 2 percent of payroll to be refunded into personal accounts.

The Social Security actuaries, in projecting intermediate rates of return for the ISAs, used the blended portfolio described on page 171 of the report of the Social Security Advisory Council. It should be noted, however, that the improved rate of return for low-income individuals under the Plan, relative to the traditional defined-benefit solution, would be sufficiently greater to allow low-income individuals still to fare better even if these intermediate rates of return from personal accounts were not achieved.

The rates of return for younger average-income beneficiaries and upper-income beneficiaries, too, would be superior under the Plan relative to a defined-benefit solution. For older workers, however, an effect could come into play at this point that also was present in the analysis of the Social Security Advisory Council's plans. The actuaries' figures incorporate the effect of PIA changes on disability benefits, and it is not possible in reviewing undifferentiated return rates to see the different effects on the retirement and disability portions of Social Security separately. Tables that separate replacement rates for the two categories reveal that the Plan would fare better across most birth years when considering the retirement portion only. The Commission was not charged with making recommendations for Social Security disability policy; and the chairs believed the effects of all such PIA changes on disability benefits would need to be noted frankly; and that legislative implementation of this Plan should not apply such PIA changes to the disability program without further study.

The progressivity achieved by the 21st Century Retirement Security Plan would mean that, to a significant extent, low-income workers would be shielded successfully from the adverse effects of benefit changes made to carve out an ISA of 2 percent. The chairs believed that the focus of benefit restraints on high-income individuals underscores the desirability of permitting additional voluntary contributions to these accounts. If these were permitted, low-income workers would have received an improved rate of return through the means of added progressivity in the traditional benefit formula, while average- to high-income workers would be able to increase their net rates of return through voluntary contributions. The unequal abilities of individuals of different income levels to take advantage of voluntary contributions is the chief reason that adding progressivity to the OASDI program is essential.

Illustrative examples reveal how the importance of the ISA portion would grow with time. The average single worker retiring at age 65 in 2030 would do notably better under the Commission's Plan, assuming intermediate rates of return, than under a traditional defined-benefit solution. If the worker chose to make additional voluntary contributions to the individual account, his advantage would increase. The worker retiring at age 67 in 2060, however, would receive fully 38 percent more under the Plan than under a traditional solution, again before counting the effects of voluntary contributions.

It should be noted, too, that these distributional effects in some respects understate the income to be provided under the Plan because each of the workers depicted would have been subject to some reduction in benefits due to not having reached normal retirement age as defined by the Plan. All four plans considered by the Commission would decrease the percentage of PIA received in early retirement and increase the delayed retirement credit. Thus, individuals retiring at normal retirement age or later would receive greater income than depicted in these examples.

In the long run, the impact of the Plan would be positive for the unified budget relative to current law. The Commission considered a worst-case scenario for short-term costs, assuming that the federal government simply would add the cost of the Social Security transition to federal borrowing and enact no offsetting measures. The additional borrowing and interest payments that would result from such a policy were included in the Commission's estimate that annual transition costs would drop to zero by 2017. If any offsets were enacted, the transition would have a positive effect earlier than this.

Additional Views

Congressional Cochairs

The recommendations in this report do not reflect the individual policy preferences of any one member of the Commission. We are greatly pleased that, despite the enormous diversity of viewpoints, members unanimously chose to set an example of bipartisan compromise instead of electing to emphasize areas of specific disagreement.

Unlike other commissions in which differences sharpen and positions harden as the discussion progresses, the sincere airing of legitimate concerns led each member of the NCRP to move beyond individually held opinions and toward a middle ground between ideological poles. As Congress confronts the multitude of issues in retirement policy reform, it will need to muster a comparable willingness to turn disparate opinions into unified recommendations.

The accompanying "additional views" are an important component of the *Final Report of the National Commission on Retirement Policy.* We believe that many members of the Commission would not have voted to support its unified recommendations had it not been for the fact that each member knew he would be permitted to file separate views.

The congressional cochairs are among the Commission members who agreed to compromise on personally held policy preferences in the interest of securing agreement. Such issues ranged from the opportunity to "roll over" ISA balances, to efforts to add progressive elements to ISAs and IRAs, to many others.

The Commission sought to expand the discussion regarding Social Security reform by considering new ideas that previously had not been analyzed fully and adequately. During the Commission's deliberations, many such innovative and interesting ideas were discussed. Some of these proposals, such as the minimum benefit provision, were included in the Plan once commissioners were satisfied by the level of analysis that had been completed. Many other ideas discussed by Commission members could not be included in the Plan, however, because the Commission was not able to obtain data on the fiscal implications of the provisions; nor was it able to answer technical concerns about the way in which these proposals would be implemented. Many of these ideas are presented in the additional views submitted by Commission members.

Although the Commission as a whole did not endorse these proposals, it does believe that such innovative options as those described in the additional views should be considered part of any final Social Security reform legislation that achieves the objectives outlined by the Commission.

It is important to remember that a comprehensive package of reform cannot remain viable after naïve substitutions of certain provisions for others. For example, the Social Security recommendations here simultaneously achieve the goals of actuarial solvency, stable annual cash-flow, targeted progressivity, and comparable treatment of successive birth cohorts. Eliminating one provision and replacing it with another that may provide an equal contribution to actuarial balance could interfere with the smoothness of annual cash flow and with distributive goals. Accordingly, policy considerations, as much as the spirit of compromise, favor the report of a comprehensive package as opposed to a menu of options, each with separate levels of support.

We trust that the additional views will be read in light of the Commission's success in achieving unanimity, and as an example of the diversity of concerns that must be melded if Congress is to enact comprehensive retirement policy reform.

Warren Batts

I was pleased to serve as a member of the NCRP. I believe its work and its bipartisan character represent the most significant advancement thus far in the continuing debate over the future of the Social Security retirement system.

One aspect of the work of the NCRP deserves special attention.

The Commission reached a unanimous conclusion, but only after vigorous debate among its members. Unanimity did not come easily, but only because the Commission members with strongly held, differing viewpoints were willing to subordinate individual opinion to collective judgment.

Further, I wish to point out, in particular, two aspects of the NCRP recommendations.

First, changes advocated by the Commission are responsive to the simple reality that the U.S. economy cannot remain vigorous without reform of the Social Security system. Moreover, reform would allow individuals and families to grow with an expanding economy, and to increase the well-being and independence to which all Americans are entitled.

Second, the recommendations of the NCRP concerning personal retirement accounts are unequivocally congruent with the protection that federal law provides individuals who participate in employer-sponsored retirement plans. To this effect, account assets remain the property of each individual and are not forfeitable; the assets are managed and invested subject to rules for fiduciaries and for the exclusive purpose of providing the individual with retirement income. Stated more simply: the money in the account belongs to the individual who earned it, to be invested and managed accordingly.

William A. Galston

The NCRP's Plan represents an important point of departure for what I hope will be a sober and searching debate about the best way to provide a decent and secure retirement for elderly Americans in the twenty-first century. Nevertheless, the Plan can be improved in some respects. For example:

☐ Instead of raising the early retirement age in tandem with the normal retirement age, I believe it would be preferable to retain the early retirement age specified in current law while adjusting the monthly payments received by early retirees to eliminate subsidies for early retirement as measured actuarially relative to normal retirement. This would help to ease the burden on demographic groups that experience lower-than-average life expectancy while maintaining the fiscal integrity of the overall system.

☐ The principle of honoring legitimate expectations is an important element of our moral understanding. This principle has special force as applied to individuals who cannot adjust easily to unexpected changes in those expectations—in the case of Social Security, individuals at or near retirement age. For this reason, I believe the effective dates of the relevant provisions of the NCRP's Plan should be adjusted so that individuals 55 or older as of the date of enactment would be held harmless relative to their expectations under current law.

☐ In addition, I believe it is crucial to stress important features of the NCRP's Plan that may be overlooked amid the controversy over our highest-profile recommendations.

☐ The Plan would adopt a more stringent and prudent definition of solvency than specified in current law—a stable trust fund ratio in perpetuity rather than balance over a 75-year cycle. This change would improve the odds that future generations would be able to rely on the expectations generated by the system.

☐ The new minimum benefit—60 percent of poverty for individuals who have worked for 20 years, rising by 2 percent per year to 100 percent for those with 40 years of work—would enhance significantly the progressivity of the system.

☐ Taken together, the various provisions of the Plan would generate increased benefits relative to current policy for low-income workers—even those who had adopted risk-averse, lower-yield investment strategies for their personal accounts.

☐ We dealt thoughtfully and responsibly with such issues as administrative costs and mandatory annuitization of personal accounts.

Estelle James

I strongly support the major thrust of the Commission's recommendations because I believe they are in the interests of the elderly as well as of the broader economy. I would like to add the following four caveats and tradeoffs, however:

1. There is the danger that the baby boom generation will suffer cuts in benefits while future generations will gain if the bend-point factors are cut faster than the buildup of the individual accounts. In my opinion, the timing of bend-point factor changes should be set to avoid this intergenerational redistribution because it does not appear warranted on the grounds of efficiency or equity. If we want to avoid deficit finance, this transition cost may require a small interim increase in contributions.

2. It is possible that, as an outcome of the political process, the early retirement age will remain lower than we recommend. In that case, I believe that actuarially fair reductions in benefits are essential. But this may result in the benefits for many early retirees falling below the poverty line. If we want to permit early retirement and we also want to prevent poverty in old age, the price again may be a small increase in contributions.

3. On average, the individual accounts should raise benefits and rates of return on Social Security contributions (assuming future financial market returns resemble past returns), but for some periods and individuals this may not be the case, considering the variability in stock market returns. To avoid low benefits for some cohorts and individuals, it may be desirable to aim at slightly higher average benefits—and this, too, would require slightly higher contributions.

4. The low allocation to the individual accounts (only two percentage points, or about $500 per year for the average worker) may lead many workers to conclude it is not worth their time and effort to think carefully about ways to invest the money. But a larger allocation may require higher contributions, if we wish to keep the social safety net provided by the remaining defined-benefit plan.

The above caveats suggest that—depending on benefit projections and early retirement age—somewhat higher contributions may be in order, especially in the short run. In considering this possibility, we should bear in mind that benefit and contribution rates in the United States are low compared to those in other industrialized countries. If we decided to move in this direction, my preference would be to keep the contribution rate unchanged but to raise the ceiling on taxable earnings, thereby increasing aggregate contributions while making the system more progressive. This would allow us to slow down the change in bend-point factors, to increase the benefit rate for everyone including early retirees, and (after, say, 2005) to allocate an additional percentage point to the individual accounts. If the returns on the individual accounts are sufficiently high, the contribution rate could be reduced in the future.

Beth Kobliner

A great deal of attention has been paid to polls that suggest young people do not believe that Social Security will provide for them as it has for their parents and grandparents. One main advantage of the NCRP Plan is the sense of ownership it would provide to Social Security participants who question the government's ability to meet future promises. The Plan, which I support, carefully balances the interests and preferences of individuals with the solvency of the Social Security system as a whole, and includes at its heart significant and vital protections for low-income Americans. I do have several concerns, however:

❑ **The public needs to understand that, with a system of individual accounts, the individual will be subject to greater market risk.** In a public defined-benefit system, the government manages market risk instead of the individual and has complete control over the distribution of benefits. Under the Commission's proposal, individuals would take on part of that risk through their ISAs in exchange for greater involvement in the process. This tradeoff should be explained clearly to the public when changes to Social Security are being discussed. Moreover, if individual accounts do become part of Social Security, every effort needs to be made to ensure that a solid base level of defined benefits remains protected in the years to come.

❑ **The public needs to understand the pros and cons of investing in individual accounts, especially with regard to equities.** Although investors in the past decade have benefited from the phenomenal expansion of the market, the market's recent volatility should remind us of this fundamental truth: We have no guarantee that the market will continue to deliver the returns of the past decade, or even the past 70 years. Under a system of ISAs, retirement savings will become partially contingent on the performance of the stock market; if the market drops, people investing in stocks will lose the money on which they would depend for retirement. Such losses would not be devastating for upper-income participants, and the Commission has worked diligently to preserve the benefits of lower-income individuals. But middle-income individuals—in our assumptions, participants earning roughly $28,000 a year—must be educated about the risk/reward tradeoffs of the stock market.

❑ **We need to protect individuals from making speculative investments they cannot absorb.** The Commission currently advocates a system that features four or five investment options, including stock index funds, a bond index fund, and a government securities fund. But the Plan goes on to envision the eventual introduction of an "increased number of investment options" along with the option of rolling over ISA money into similar, individually held private accounts. As the number of choices increases, adequate protections—such as diversification guidelines or rules for liquidity—must be in place, and administrative costs must be kept to a strict minimum. Otherwise, the temptation of speculative investment may lead participants to lose the money on which they would rely for their retirement years.

❑ **We need to help middle-income Americans to save more.** The Commission acknowledged the importance of encouraging middle-class

Americans to save more and expressed interest in concrete proposals (including tax credits or government matching programs) to help us to accomplish this goal. The Commission's Plan, however, limits itself to recommending that fully deductible IRAs be extended (like Roth IRAs) to couples that earn up to $160,000 and individuals that earn up to $110,000 (from current levels of $50,000 and $30,000, respectively). Although simplification is a worthy goal, my concern is that this kind of initiative would favor the transfer of wealth from the public coffers to people who are well-off already (and who need little incentive to save) without offering any proposals to help the less affluent. I think it is important that this discussion be continued by Congress and by future commissions of this nature.

Robert C. Pozen

I believe the NCRP's Plan is a thoughtful effort to better assure Americans' retirement income adequacy into the twenty-first century. The proposal does so by focusing on all three elements of retirement income—Social Security, employer-sponsored retirement programs, and individual retirement savings—instead of focusing on just one of them. I believe that retirement income adequacy will be achieved only when all three elements of retirement savings are in a proper balance. The Commission's Plan would go a long way toward providing such balance.

The Plan is not without its flaws, however. Specifically, I am concerned about the approach it takes with regard to personal accounts. Although I appreciate the administrative issues, I believe the Plan strips away much of what would make such personal accounts attractive—features like broad investment choice, immediacy of investment of payroll contributions, the ability to change investments frequently, and, perhaps most important, the assurance that significant educational efforts are being made to inform participants about investing the money in their personal accounts.

I therefore believe it would be a mistake to rely solely on a government-run personal account program; such a program would have to be built from scratch. I estimate it would take at least three years to build such a program and that it ultimately would require as many as 100,000 new government employees to operate it. Therefore, I believe the program would be considerably more flexible if we also took advantage of existing programs—such as participant-directed 401(k) plans and individual retirement accounts—as a vehicle for the personal accounts.

To be more specific, I would enable participants who so desire to opt out of the government-run personal account based on the TSP model and into a private market personal account. I assume this account would be limited to 2 percent of the participant's Social Security contribution, as does the Commission's proposal. To simplify the administration of such private market personal accounts, such an opt-out would be limited to the following already existing types of retirement accounts:

☐ A participant-directed 401(k) plan that met the requirements of ERISA §404(c), but only if the employer sponsoring such a plan permitted the private market personal accounts to be maintained under that 401(k) plan; or

☐ A Social Security IRA (SIRA), but only if the financial institution sponsoring the SIRA agreed to maintain it in accordance with ERISA §404(c), as explained below.

In the case of the 401(k) plan, the employer simply would contribute the 2 percent incrementally to the plan instead of forwarding it to the Department of the Treasury. This could be done on the same time schedule as the 401(k) plan, for example—monthly or quarterly. In the case of the SIRA alternative, the employer would continue to forward the 2 percent to the Department of the Treasury, but a participant who opted out of the Federal Thrift Plan model would obtain a tax *credit* of equal amount in order to avoid overpayment of Social Security taxes. The participant would qualify for the tax credit by making one annual contribution to an SIRA at a financial institution and would use the tax credit either to reduce withholding taxes or to obtain a tax refund. Under either option, the employer therefore would take on little or no additional administrative responsibility.

Such an opt-out would allow participants to choose among a broader range of investment alternatives than permitted under the Federal Thrift Plan model while still subjecting those accounts to the safeguards of Department of Labor regulations under ERISA §404(c). Under those regulations, a plan must offer at least three diversified "core" options, each of which has materially different risk and return characteristics. These core options would be similar to the three options under the Federal Thrift Plan. A 404(c) plan also could offer additional investment options; most 404(c) plans offer between 10 and 12 investment options, including the 3 core options. Any financial institution sponsoring an SIRA would be required to distribute an educational brochure about those options to participants designed to enable them to make intelligent investment decisions.

The flaw in the proposal regarding the personal accounts does not negate the power of the proposal in its attempt to balance the three elements of the retirement savings system properly. The personal account provision, however, in many ways is the cornerstone of the NCRP Plan—the link between provisions relating to Social Security on the one hand and the employer-sponsored retirement and individual retirement savings proposal on the other. I therefore believe Congress should spend more time in considering the administrative and investment issues involved with personal accounts as well as the significant potential benefits offered by private-sector accounts.

Dallas Salisbury

The Employee Benefit Research Institute (EBRI) is a nonpartisan, nonlobbying organization. As a result, I normally do not agree to serve on groups like the NCRP. What attracted me was the chairmen's insistence that, to be worthwhile, we had to reach a consensus or we might as well go home. They made the point that

Congress either acts or punts, and that we should do the same. As a result, we were able to recommend a package, even though many individual elements would not have been approved on a stand-alone basis. In addition, because we did not have the resources that Congress does, some of the recommendations could use further analysis. The most significant:

❒ **Spousal treatment.** The NCRP Plan would reduce the value of Social Security spousal benefits from 50 percent of the primary earner's benefit to 33 percent. This is a major change that could use detailed analysis to provide guidance on the appropriate phase-in period.

❒ **Minimum benefit provision.** By further reducing Social Security's link between earnings records and program benefits, this reform could be expected to place a disincentive on work effort—especially for marginal workers, those at the threshold between earning the minimum benefit and the benefits provided for the rest of the population. This is a major departure from current law, on which we did not undertake analysis of behavioral consequences. The same is true for changes in the benefit formulas: AIME and PIA.

❒ **Raising the retirement ages.** The Commission's recommendation to raise the early retirement age to 65 and the normal retirement age to 70 recognizes improvements in life expectancy, but we did not analyze fully the implications for workers in physically demanding jobs, the integration with disability insurance, or employer plan retirement age policies of public and private employers.

❒ **Implementing individual accounts.** Large and uncertain amounts of revenue and time would be involved in establishing computer systems, offices, and personnel to handle 15 times as many participants as the largest defined-contribution plan record keeper. Social Security covers 83.5 times as many people as the TSP. Social Security would hold at least 7.0 times the number of individual accounts currently held by active 401(k) participants and at least 4.0 times the number of all employment-based defined-contribution accounts combined. With nearly 6 million employers still providing wage information to Social Security once per year on paper, the transition time should not be underestimated. Conservatively, any type of universal individual account program could take 10 years to put in place and require a staff of more than 100,000. Great care should be taken to do it right, and not to make too many promises to the people.

I thank the Commission and its staff for providing me with this unique opportunity.

Josephine "Josie" Tsao

The Commission's stated objective was to improve retirement savings by providing increased opportunities for saving, simplifying the rules governing retirement plans, improving pension portability, and modernizing pension provisions to reflect changes in the workforce. We made a number of important recommendations to achieve this objective. I believe more needs to be done, however, to meet these goals. In particular, Congress should consider additional ways in which to make defined-benefit plans a more attractive component of retirement savings. One way could be by giving employers additional flexibility to coordinate their defined-benefit and defined-contribution plans and offer employees choices that maximize the best features of both arrangements. Two specific proposals would assist in achieving these goals:

1. **Allow employers with excess defined-benefit plan assets to use assets in excess of a determined percentage of current liabilities to fund their contributions to their defined-contribution plans.** The excess assets could be used only to fund employer contributions made on behalf of employees who also participated in the defined-benefit plan. This change would encourage employers to fund their defined-benefit plans aggressively and keep them from becoming inhibited from using conservative funding assumptions because they would know that, if they got into a situation in which there were more than enough assets than needed to meet all future benefit obligations, they could use those assets to fund other retirement savings plans. Congress recognized that the inability to use excess assets for other purposes represented a significant disincentive to employers' willingness to offer defined-benefit plans when it allowed certain excess assets to be used to fund retiree health obligations. Although this is a beneficial provision, it is limited to those employers that offer retiree health benefits and have a number of conditions attached. Employers should be allowed to use these assets to make contributions to retirement savings plans that offer features valued by employees, including portability and control over investment decisions.

2. **Allow employers to offer their employees the opportunity to transfer the value of their accrued benefit in a defined-benefit pension plan into the employers' defined-contribution plans.** If the employee chose to make this transfer, the optional forms of benefits provided by the defined-benefit plan would not have to be maintained in the defined-contribution plan. Such transfers would facilitate the concept of "partial retirement." By transferring the value of their accrued benefit from a defined-benefit plan to a defined-contribution plan, older workers who were eligible for retirement but wished to continue part-time employment would be able to withdraw amounts from the defined-contribution plan while continuing to work. Conversely, participants also could transfer their defined-contribution plan account balances into the employer's defined-benefit plan. This proposal would allow employees to choose the form of retirement savings that met their objectives. If they wanted investment control, portability, and the opportunity to make in-service

withdrawals, they could move into the defined-contribution plan. If they preferred a guaranteed benefit, payable as an annuity and insured by the government, the defined-benefit plan would be more attractive. The government should encourage—not restrict—this type of flexibility. Finally, the Plan is consistent with current policy initiatives that would ease restrictions on removing optional forms of benefits, improve pension portability, and allow self-direction of investments within cash balance plans.

These two changes would encourage employers to offer plans with both defined-benefit and defined-contribution plan features and to fund them generously. It would give employees access to both types of plans and the flexibility to choose the mix that best met their needs. Truly, a retirement system for the twenty-first century.

David M. Walker

I, along with every other member of the NCRP, voted in favor of adopting this Plan. This is a minor miracle in light of the diversity of the Commission members, the complexity of this subject, and the emotions that can be associated with it. The unanimous vote is a tribute as well to the work of the staff of the Commission members and CSIS.

Although I have concerns regarding some of the individual recommendations contained in this report and am disappointed at the failure to incorporate certain other recommendations herein, I believe that the recommendations, when viewed as a package, represent a significant improvement over the status quo. At the same time, I believe that the following personal comments are appropriate.

Any comprehensive reform of the Social Security system should be designed to maintain a sound, certain, secure, and sustainable base level of defined benefit that is protected against inflation and targeted to provide greater replacement rates for lower- and lower middle–income workers. Any ISA element should come in addition to, instead of in lieu of, the base level of defined benefit. Reforms should be designed to have little or no impact on current and near-term retirees. In addition, any significant reform elements should be phased in over reasonable transition periods in order to assure fairness (that is, time for individuals to adjust) and feasibility (that is, implementation of any ISA element).

With regard to possible omissions from the report, I believe that additional emphasis should be placed on expanding employer and other collective pension and retirement savings arrangements, revising minimum participation standards in light of the changing workforce, enhancing women's pension equity and security, and preserving retirement savings, including IRA savings, for retirement income purposes.

Finally, real retirement security requires that individuals have an adequate stream of income throughout their retirement years and access to affordable healthcare. As a result, even though this Commission focused on retirement income security issues, ultimately, it will become necessary for employers and policymakers to focus on a range of other health care and employment issues in order to assure that individuals have a reasonable standard of living in their retirement years. In addition, employers, government, and other parties need to do more to help individuals to help themselves to plan, save, and invest for retirement.